# ENTER A FREE MAN

# ENTER
# A FREE MAN

## TOM STOPPARD

ff

*faber and faber*

LONDON · BOSTON

First published in 1968
by Faber and Faber Limited
3 Queen Square London WC1N 3AU
Reprinted 1971, 1973, 1977 and 1981
Reissued in 1986
Reprinted 1991

Printed in England by Clays Ltd, St Ives plc

A CIP record for this book is available
from the British Library

ISBN 0-571-08794-9

In an earlier version, under the title *A Walk on the Water*, this play was first performed in a television production by Rediffusion in November, 1963.

The first London performance of *Enter A Free Man* was at the St. Martin's Theatre on March 28th, 1968. The cast was as follows:

| | |
|---|---|
| George Riley | MICHAEL HORDERN |
| Persephone | MEGS JENKINS |
| Linda | VANESSA FORSYTH |
| Harry | ROLAND CURRAM |
| Florence | MARIA CHARLES |
| Carmen | LIAM GAFFNEY |
| Able | ROY HOLDER |
| Brown | KENNETH MC CLELLAN |

*Directed by* FRITH BANBURY

*Designed by* REECE PEMBERTON

*Lighting by* JOHN B. READ

# CHARACTERS

GEORGE RILEY

PERSEPHONE

LINDA

HARRY

ABLE

CARMEN

FLORENCE

BROWN

# ACT ONE

*Stage Right is the living-room of* RILEY'S *home . . . a dining-table with chairs, a settee, a grandfather clock, a portrait of the Queen, a transistor radio (the only thing that does not look vaguely out of date). Everything is spick and span. There are lots of potted plants, on sills, shelves and tables, and almost everywhere where there is a plant there is some plumbing above it, quite discreet. Stairs to the bedrooms can be seen beyond the door.*

PERSEPHONE *is responsible for the tidiness. She is matronly, plump, plain, nice, vague, usually vaguely distracted. She is a great duster and emptier of ash-trays. Her daughter* LINDA *is in pyjamas. She is eighteen, self-assured, at least on the surface, and can be as cruel or warm as she feels like being. She is never sentimental, and often anti-sentiment: sharp, abrasive, cool, when her guard is up, and rather childlike when it drops.*

*Stage Left is the bar, the public bar of a slightly old-fashioned unfashionable pub in what is probably a seedy urban suburb.*

*The two playing areas blend into one another at Downstage Centre but they have no geographical relationship.* CARMEN *the barman is middle-aged and big, taciturn but in fact warm, tough-looking but curiously ineffectual.* HARRY *is thirty-odd, flashy, sharp, well dressed, cheaply rakish.*

ABLE *is a young callow sailor, almost gormless.*

BROWN *is almost anonymous—meek, colourless—a man in a pub, minding his own business.*

RILEY *is a smallish untidy figure in a crumpled suit (when he appears)—a soiled fifty with a certain education somewhere in the past: it gives him a tattered dignity now. He is certainly not mad but he is definitely odd. Unsinkable, despite the slow leak.*

*Before the curtain rises; "Rule Britannia". The music fades to nothing as the lights come up on the home.*

*At home;* PERSEPHONE *and* LINDA. LINDA *in pyjamas.*

PERSEPHONE: You'd better get dressed, Linda. We don't want

another row when your father gets in.

LINDA: He won't get back till late . . . meatless Saturday for George Riley, the man who's on his way . . . to the pub on the corner.

(*The lights come up slowly on the bar.*)

(*In the bar;* CARMEN *behind the bar.*)

PERSEPHONE: Well, why shouldn't he go to the pub? At least he meets people.

LINDA: How do you know? I bet he's just another lonely feller having a quiet drink. The point is, what's he like? I mean when we can't see him. He's got to be different—I mean you wouldn't even *know* me if you could see me——

(ABLE *enters, downstage of the bar, carrying a letter and writing-paper. He collects a glass of beer from the bar and goes slowly to the corner table and sits, writing letter.*)

PERSEPHONE: Come on, Linda.

(*She leaves the room and goes off towards the kitchen.*)

LINDA: And that goes for everyone. There's two of everyone.

(*The gent* (BROWN) *enters downstage of bar and sits on stool, reading newspaper.*)

You see you need that

(HARRY *enters upstage of bar, looks about impatiently.*)

and if the two of him's the same, I mean if he's the same in the pub as he is with us, then he's had it.

(RILEY *enters with a flourish, but his entrance makes no impact.*)

RILEY: Enter a free man!

LINDA: Poor old Dad . . .

HARRY: It's him again.

RILEY: Free as the proverbial bird.

(PERSEPHONE *reappears at the home door.*)

PERSEPHONE: Linda. (*Goes off and upstairs.*)

(*The lights on the home start to fade.*)

LINDA (*rising and going off upstairs*): You'll have to do something about him, you know . . .

RILEY: Unashamed I have left her.

LINDA: Before I'm old and ugly.

RILEY: A good woman I daresay, in many ways a fine woman—

in many ways a terrible liability. Who'll drink to that? A toast.

(*No reaction. He pauses in the vacuum . . . the living-room has faded.*)

What time do you open?

ABLE: Morning, Mr. Riley. . . .

RILEY (*ignoring him; to* BROWN): Good lord, it's my old C.O., isn't it?

BROWN (*nervously*): I don't think so.

RILEY: I saved your life at Monte Casino—that's worth a drink!

BROWN: I'm afraid——

RILEY (*calls*): A foaming tankard on the Colonel.

(CARMEN *takes little or no notice.*)

BROWN: I don't believe——

RILEY (*dismissing him equably*): Just as you like. (*To* ABLE.) Thank God for the British Navy.

ABLE: Hello, Mr. Riley . . .

RILEY: At ease, carry on smoking.

ABLE: Oh—have one?

RILEY: Why, yes—I think I might.

(ABLE *offers and lights a cigarette.*)

HARRY (*to* CARMEN): She won't get here for next year's Derby, never mind the one o'clock . . . I'll give her five minutes. If I'm gone, tell her the same time tomorrow.

RILEY: I don't know where to start.

ABLE: What?

RILEY: Free as air. Walked out with my toothbrush and a ten-bob note, and I don't know where to start. (*Indicating* ABLE's *notepaper.*) What have you got there?

ABLE: Well, it's this letter, Mr. Riley—I don't know how to . . . I'm not very good at . . .

RILEY: Who's it to?

ABLE: Well, it's this girl, you see. I met her at this dance. I thought you might be able to . . .

(RILEY *has already taken up the letter.*)

RILEY: "Carissima Silvana . . ." (*Pause.*) Where was this dance?

ABLE: Naples.

RILEY: "Carissima Silvana . . . I'm sorry I didn't write before

11

but I put it off till we got back on Monday. I've been
thinking about you, though. Well, as you can see, we got
back all right and I've got ten days before we report back. I
don't know where we'll be going but I'm keeping my
fingers crossed for Naples. I hope your shoe's all right——"
(RILEY *looks up inquiringly.*)

ABLE: Her heel came off.

RILEY: ". . . I hope your shoe's all right. Well, I just wanted to
say I had a nice time with you, the best time I had on the
trip, and I've been thinking about you. I'm sorry the photo
is a bit blurred. The other bloke is Dave Collins, you
remember him. . . ." (*Looks up.*) Is that all?

ABLE: It's not very good, is it?

RILEY: Take a note. (*Starts dictating, pacing.*) Dear Silvana,
please try to forget me. I have just met a man in a pub
whose example stands as a warning against even the most
casual relationship with young women. A thing like that
could end in disaster—twenty-five years of dead
domesticity, fatal to a man of creative spirit—only today,
after much loss of time and dignity. . . . (*He has travelled to
the bar: to* HARRY *and* CARMEN.) Walked out with my
toothbrush and a ten-bob note. (*To* CARMEN.) A pint of
half-and-half. (*To* HARRY.) I was driven to it, you see. Do
you think I did the right thing?

HARRY: What?

RILEY: Leaving her.

HARRY: Who?

RILEY: My wife.

HARRY: Where?

RILEY: What? At home.

HARRY: Left her at home?

RILEY (*irritated*): No—I *left* her. Walked out.

HARRY: Never.

RILEY: I told you.

HARRY: What—Percy?

RILEY: Persephone is her name, if you don't mind. However,
yes I have. Man is born free and——

HARRY: Walked out on her again? Where's your stuff?

12

RILEY (*slapping his pocket with a smile*): Here. I've got
   something in here that will open doors to me, Harry.

CARMEN (*with* RILEY'*s drink*): Two and tuppence.

RILEY: Two and tuppence for a pint of half-and-half. Half beer,
   half water. Times change, Carmen, my old barman.
   (*He tosses down a ten-shilling note and turns back to* BROWN
   *and stands in front of him regarding him.*)
   I'd say you were a man who could understand.

BROWN: I beg your pardon?

RILEY: Granted. I have left my wife.

CARMEN (*from the bar*): Now then——

RILEY: I wanted you to know that. . . . Left her. My wife. You
   married?

CARMEN: Mr. Riley——

RILEY: Give me your honest opinion. What would you have
   done in my position?

BROWN: I don't really know what your position was.

RILEY: Of course you don't. How could you? I'm an inventor.

CARMEN: Your change.

RILEY: Keep it.

CARMEN: Seven and tenpence.
   (*Small pause.*)

RILEY (*getting up*): I'll owe it to you. I'll be worth thousands in
   a short while.

CARMEN: We close at three.

RILEY (*calling up to* HARRY): A man is born free and everywhere
   he is in chains. Who said that?

ABLE: Houdini?

RILEY (*turning*): Who?

ABLE: —dini.

RILEY: Houdini. No.

ABLE: Give up.

RILEY (*turning back to* HARRY): Still wasting your life, Harry?

HARRY: No, I'm waiting to see if my horse comes in before my
   pools come up.

RILEY: Gambling. The opiate of the common herd.

HARRY: For eight draws on a wet Saturday you can call me
   common, I can stand it. Filthy rich and common with it,

13

that's my idea of living. You can come and watch me through the palace railings, blowing on my soup.

RILEY: You see? Dreams. Diversions to keep the mob happy. It's the Government, you see.

HARRY: I always suspected it.

RILEY: It's the truth. The government's taking a tip from the Romans. When the place was declining and falling round their ears, you know what the Romans did?

HARRY: No?

RILEY: Bread and circuses. To take the mob's mind off it. Same thing now, only it's football. Football drugs them, keeps them hoping. And the government knows it.

HARRY: Oh, it knows it.

(ABLE *to bar, for "one more, same again".)*

RILEY: You're right. Because if the mob didn't have its circus you know what would happen? They'd rush 'em! Up from the Elephant, over Westminster Bridge, surround the Houses of Parliament and string 'em up. That's the whole point of electing an M.P.—you've got to have someone to string up as a last resort. (*Pose.*) Gentlemen! It's football or anarchy.

ABLE: It's cricket now.

RILEY: What?

ABLE: Cricket.

RILEY: True. (*Thought.*) But these things take time to grow. If cricket went on till Christmas, you know who would be ruling the country?

ABLE: Who?

RILEY: You would.

ABLE: I never look at it that way.

RILEY: Just as the mob is getting restive, football comes back, nips revolution in the bud. Have you noticed how football starts earlier and finishes later every year?

ABLE: No.

RILEY: Well, it does. It's the government. They know, you see.

HARRY: They do.

RILEY: So you can see why, can't you?

14

HARRY: I can.

RILEY: It's the Government.

HARRY: They're no fools.

RILEY (*with scorn*): Dreams! The illusion of something for nothing. No wonder the country is going to the dogs. Personal enterprise sacrificed to bureaucracy. No pride, no patriotism. The erosion of standards, the spread of mediocrity, the decline of craftsmanship and the betrayal of the small inventor.

HARRY: It's terrible really. I blame youth.

CARMEN: Education.

HARRY: The Church is out of touch.

CARMEN: The family is not what it was.

HARRY: It's the power of the unions.

CARMEN: The betrayal of the navy.

HARRY: Ban the bomb.

CARMEN: Spare the rod.

HARRY: I'm all right, Jack.

CARMEN: The little man goes to the wall.

HARRY: Supermarkets.

CARMEN: Everything's plastic.

HARRY: Country's going to the dogs. What happened to our greatness?

RILEY: Look at the Japanese!

HARRY: Look at the Japanese!

RILEY: The Japanese look after the small inventor!

HARRY: All Japanese inventors are small.

CARMEN: They're a small people.

HARRY: Very small. Short.

RILEY: The little man!

HARRY: The little people!

RILEY: Look at the transistor!

HARRY: Very small.

RILEY: Japanese!

CARMEN: Gurkhas are short.

HARRY: But exceedingly brave for their size.

CARMEN: Fearless.

RILEY (*furiously*): What are you talking about!

HARRY: Good luck!

RILEY: Oh yes—luck, leave it to luck. But luck is not for us inventors.

HARRY: You're right.

RILEY: Of course I'm right. Because we rise above it, we don't submit to the common decay. We have minds, I think therefore I am!

ABLE: I've been meaning to ask you about that, Mr. Riley——

RILEY: A man must resist. A man must stand apart, make a clean break on his own two feet! Faith is the key—faith in oneself. (*Producing out of his pocket an envelope which he waves about.*) I have in here a little idea—one of many—that will take me away from all this. I'm saying good-bye to it all, Harry, just as I said good-bye to Persephone.

HARRY: It rings a bell. Let's have a look at it.

RILEY: What the creative mind needs is respect for its independence.

HARRY: Exactly! Respect. That's what we've got for you. We all have. Right, Carmen?

CARMEN: What?

HARRY: You see—respect. You've been coming in here, and we like it. Raises the tone. Right, Carmen?

CARMEN: Eh?

HARRY: Because of what? Because we're common. I mean, what have we got to give the world? Nothing. But you're—well, you're a genius! An inventor! You're a clever bloke, sitting there in your workshop, pioneering you might say, from your blood and your sweat for the lot of your fellow man.

RILEY: The lot of my fellow man!

HARRY: It's people like you who made this country great.

RILEY: You've got something there, Harry. That's very good.

HARRY: I had to say it.

RILEY: Thank you, Harry.

HARRY: *Able* thinks you're somebody—don't you?

ABLE: What?

HARRY: Don't you think George here is a clever bloke?

ABLE: 'Course he's a clever bloke. He's an inventor, isn't he?

HARRY: My very point. An inventor. That's your job. Amazing.

16

I don't know if you've ever thought, George, but if you took away everything in the world that had to be invented, there'd be nothing left except a lot of people getting rained on.

RILEY (*excitedly*): You're right! Progress is the child of invention! . . . (*Soberly.*) Harry, I have been touched by what you have said. (*He brandishes his envelope.*) My own resources are limited, but simplicity is the hardest thing to achieve—the simple idea that is a revolution. And I have achieved it, Harry. I would like you to have the honour of being the first to see it.

HARRY: Oh, I'm very honoured, George. I'll remember this.
(RILEY *opens the envelope and takes out a smaller, ordinary letter-envelope. He hands this to* HARRY, *who inspects it and turns it over dumbly.*)
Yes. . . . Yes, I can see this going over very big. A lovely job. A nice piece of work. An envelope. But—well, George, I must confess to a slight sense of—how should I put it?——

CARMEN: Disappointment——

HARRY: Disappointment. Yes, disappointment. An envelope—oh, I'm not saying it's not good, but it's not new, George, not new. An invention is better if it's new.

RILEY: You haven't noticed. Look at it. Something's different. You see? Gum on both sides of the flap! You see what that means?

HARRY: Yeah, yeah . . . what?

RILEY: You can use it twice.
(HARRY *stands up. Walks round his stool, speechless with admiration and wonder.* RILEY *watches him expectantly.*)

HARRY: Genius . . . genius. . . .

RILEY: You've got it. An envelope you can use twice. For instance, I write you a letter. I use one side, and then *you*—turn it inside out, write my address on it—and there's your gum on the flap!

HARRY (*almost beyond words*): Simplicity. The simplicity of it. First the wheel, now this.

RILEY: You like it?

17

HARRY: Like it? It's genius, that's what it is. Millions of envelopes every day, people writing 'em, getting 'em, spending tharsands of pounds, tharsands and tharsands—and you—with a master stroke—slash their expenditure by half. Just like that!

RILEY: It's a small thing.

HARRY: Ho yes! Yes, yes, a small thing. And so is the bath plug. Simple. Obvious. But the boy who latched on to that—you know where he is now?

RILEY: Where?

HARRY: In his solid gold bath-tub, that's where. Sitting up to here in champagne, taking his plug in and out— Hold, hold!

(*This warning is an apparent suspicion of* BROWN *who comes up to the bar.*)

RILEY: What?

HARRY (*a jerk of his head at* BROWN): Walls have ears.

RILEY: Eh?

HARRY: Shh! Industrial spies—they're everywhere.

(BROWN *orders, nods pleasantly at* RILEY.)

BROWN: Rousseau——

RILEY (*coldly*): I'm sorry. I don't believe we have been introduced.

BROWN: "Man is born free and——"

RILEY (*shouting*): Keep out of this—keep your distance.

(BROWN *retires.*)

(*To* HARRY.) Yes?

HARRY: What?

RILEY: Do you think they'll buy it?

HARRY: Who?

RILEY: Imperial Stationery—they're the biggest——

HARRY: Buy it? They'll have that envelope off you before you can say "how much?".

RILEY (*excitedly*): You're right! I know you're right. I said so, didn't I?

HARRY: It's a crying shame, isn't it?

RILEY: What is?

HARRY: Listen—work it out for yourself. Now here's this firm

18

—does nothing all day but makes envelopes you can use once——

RILEY: And writing-pads.

HARRY: Naturally, naturally— Now an envelope you can use *twice*—I mean, God help them! The poor bleeders took years of research, years of research, George, to produce an envelope you can use once.

RILEY: And sticky labels.

HARRY: Gummed on one side only! You can see how their minds work. All they think about is profits.

RILEY: Shocking.

HARRY: And you know what they're working on now? Half-envelopes. You've got to buy two to post a letter.

RILEY: That's clever.

HARRY: Yes, it's clever. Now think George, if your idea gets around someone else is liable to make them—right? So what happens? Shops flooded with envelopes you can use twice. So will people buy Imperial?—you're kidding. They'll buy——

RILEY: Envelopes with gum on both sides of the flap. My envelopes.

HARRY. What a brain. Like lightning.

(CARMEN *has been listening amused, but*——)

CARMEN (*worried*): Harry——

HARRY (*to* CARMEN): Belt up——

RILEY: But that means . . . What does it mean, Harry?

HARRY: It means they'll have those rights off you in two shakes of a cheque-book. They'll shove a gin in your left hand, a pen in your right, a cigar in your gob, and there you'll be—helpless. Fifty quid in your pocket and bang goes your idea into the safe. And that's where it'll stay till it's eaten by the mice.

RILEY: They won't use it?

HARRY: Never.

RILEY: Never?

HARRY: Never.

RILEY: The bastards! Typical! Big business! How could they do this to me? I'll sue them!

19

HARRY: You haven't sold it yet.

RILEY (*in excitement he wanders round the bar and back towards* ABLE): I'll sell it first and then I'll sue them. Able, what are you smoking? I'll get myself a lawyer.

ABLE (*proffering cigarette*): What's up, Mr. Riley?

HARRY (*bemused to* CARMEN): He's fantastic.

CARMEN: Lay off.

HARRY: He's fantastic.

CARMEN: Now look——

HARRY: No—you'd be playing into their hands, George. They've got more lawyers than you've had breakfasts.

RILEY: Ah. Yes. A point. What chance has the little man got?

HARRY: Oh, he's got a lot of chance, George. Don't forget, they were little men once. They must have started in a small way.

RILEY: That's true. What should I do, then?

HARRY: Do what they did. Fight them on their own terms.

RILEY: Do you think so?

HARRY: I'm certain of it. It's your only chance.

RILEY: I don't follow exactly.

HARRY: But you need a partner.

RILEY: Yes. . . . That's true. . . . I've always wanted a partner.

HARRY: I mean . . . suppose we—you and me——

RILEY: You . . . and——

HARRY: No, no, we couldn't.

RILEY: Yes we could!

HARRY: I don't know.

RILEY: Harry! Harry! Please be my partner, Harry! That's what I've always wanted—a partner! I'm no good by myself.

HARRY (*thoughtfully*): Fifty-fifty. Shares. Yes . . . yes, it'd be worth a fortune. My capital and your brains. . . . That's how they all started.

RILEY (*hopping about in excitement*): That's it! If we don't do it now we'll never do it!

HARRY: It might be worth a try——

RILEY: It is! Partners! I've got a partner! (*Arrives at* ABLE, *slaps him on the back.*) We're going to do it!

ABLE: Do what?

20

(*A helpless pause.*)

HARRY: We're going to make our own.

(RILEY *returns hesitantly.*)

RILEY: What?

HARRY: Yes—it's the only way for a man like you, George. Stand by yourself. Compete. Drive them out of business.

CARMEN: Harry——

HARRY: Same again.

RILEY (*almost giggling with fear*): Harry—you don't mean—I mean—don't they have *factories* and things?

HARRY (*hurt*): Well, how do you like that? Here I am offering you your big chance and all I get is a lot of petty objections. It's a bit hard.

RILEY: But——

HARRY: No, I'm disappointed in you, George, I am really. I thought you'd jump at a chance like this.

ABLE: Go on, Mr. Riley, take a chance. A bloke like you can't fail, I mean.

RILEY: Harry——

ABLE: Don't be so modest, Mr. Riley—a man like you——

HARRY: He's right. He's put his nicotined finger right on it. You're too modest about your brain, George. I mean, how many inventors are there round about? You're practically unique. The last of a breed. Think of all the inventors you know and see if they aren't all dead. And, George, I'll tell you something for nothing. Modesty is a fine thing—I admire it. But not in business, George. This is every man for himself. Survival of the fittest. Dog eat dog. Sink or swim. That's how things are in this cruel commercial world. It offends a man of my sensitive nature. Able will tell you the same thing.

ABLE: Well——

HARRY: You're too modest, George.

ABLE: You're too modest, Mr. Riley.

(*Pause.*)

RILEY: You think so?

HARRY: No question. I'm certain of it. Able is certain of it. He's got a great admiration for you, George.

ABLE: I've got a great admiration for you, Mr. Riley. Caw, to think one day I'll be telling my kids—George Riley?—he was a pal of mine—I used to drink with him—he was one of the nicest blokes——

HARRY: *He* isn't dead yet.

ABLE: It'll be like all those blokes turning up saying how they used to make Hitler's bed in the papers.

HARRY: Don't confuse him.

CARMEN (*bringing* HARRY's *drink*): Harry don't be a——

HARRY: Cheers.

CARMEN: It's gone twelve.

HARRY (*looks round*): Where the hell has she got to?

RILEY (*dreamily*): It's possible—oh, it's more than likely. . . . Yes, yes I think so. I knew it in my bones really. I knew it was only a matter of time. I had it in me, you see. . . . And there'll be no going back—this is the last time. . . . Dry your eyes and be a man, woman— Man must go and woman must weep. . . . What are you smoking, Able?
(ABLE *gives* RILEY *a cigarette.* CARMEN *goes back to the bar with* HARRY's *money.* HARRY *follows him for his change.*)

HARRY: Look at them. They're going to be a terrible disappointment to each other one day.

RILEY (*to* ABLE): We'll corner the market. We'll make them in millions——

ABLE: What are you making anyway?

RILEY: Envelopes with gum on both sides of the flap.
(ABLE *stares thoughtfully ahead.*)

CARMEN (*almost angry*): Harry——

HARRY: Yeah, I know. George, I've got to be going.

RILEY (*coming over*): Harry, shake hands.
(*They shake.*)
We have to discuss this further.

HARRY: Think about it. Examine it from every angle. You may change your mind.

RILEY: Never. The die is cast.

HARRY: Think about it harder.

RILEY: I shall, Harry, I shall. Shall we say same time tomorrow.

HARRY: I'll be showing my face in for a minute. (*He starts to leave.*)

CARMEN (*doubtfully*): Listen—you're not *really*——?

HARRY: Tell her—I couldn't wait.

CARMEN: All right—but——

HARRY: Same time tomorrow.

RILEY: Farewell—partner!

> (HARRY *goes.* CARMEN *disappears behind the bar.*)
> A partnership—my goodness—did you hear that? I'm walking now, I'm on my way, committed—I'm walking and I'm not going to stop . . . I can't wait to see their faces. It came to me in a flash . . . I was just sitting there thinking. . . .
> (*His wanderings have brought him to* BROWN. RILEY *whips his envelope out of sight and stares at* BROWN, *who becomes uncomfortable about it.*)
> How much did you hear?

BROWN: Hear?

RILEY: Don't play the innocent with me because I can see right through you.

BROWN: I don't think I follow.

RILEY: Company spy!

BROWN: What?

RILEY: You're from Imperial Stationery.

BROWN: From where?

RILEY: I see. Well, we have ways of making you people talk. (*Barks.*) What's your name?

BROWN (*jumps*): Brown.

RILEY (*hollow laugh*): Brown! Oh dear, oh dear! An amateur! Brown . . . ! (*Swings round and barks.*) You'll have to do better than that.

BROWN: I don't know what you're talking about.

RILEY: I suppose you've had me watched—is that it?

BROWN: Watched? What for?

> (ABLE *wanders over to join the game which is no game to* RILEY.)

ABLE: He's not a spy, is he?

RILEY: Why do you say that?

ABLE: Well—he doesn't look like a spy.

23

RILEY (*severely*): What a ridiculous observation. You don't know the first thing about espionage. A good agent must be inconspicuous—without that he might as well go home. Now *I'm* not inconspicuous. *You're* not inconspicuous. But *he* stands out a mile.

ABLE (*to* BROWN): What do you say to that?

RILEY: We're on to something here.

ABLE: We'll have to break down his cover.

BROWN: I assure you——

ABLE (*excitedly*): Maybe he's got the place bugged!

BROWN: I really——

ABLE: Microphones! Look for secret microphones! (*Snatches the man's buttonhole and tosses it aside. Looks under the table.*)

BROWN: Stop it—how dare you!

ABLE: Destroy the tapes!

RILEY: Out with it, Smith!

BROWN: Brown.

RILEY: Give me that tape.

BROWN (*shrill*): Leave me alone!

RILEY (*calmly decisive*): All right. (*Murmurs to* ABLE.) Give me the cigarettes. Psychology. Picked it up in the war. (*He becomes friendly.*) Cigarette?

BROWN: I don't smoke.

RILEY: Mind if I carry on?

(BROWN *is relieved at the new tone. He relaxes.*)

BROWN: No. Please do.

RILEY: Take a seat.

BROWN: Thank you.

(RILEY *lights cigarette and returns box of cigarettes to* ABLE.)

RILEY (*pleasantly*): Tell us about yourself, Green.

BROWN (*carefully*): My name is Brown——

RILEY (*smoothly*): Good, good. . . . And where do you live?

BROWN: 14 Mafeking Villas.

RILEY: Married?

BROWN: Yes.

RILEY: Children?

BROWN: No.

RILEY: How long have you been with Imperial?

BROWN: I sell students' textbooks.

RILEY: Come, come, we're all friends here. Have a drink. (*Shouts.*) Carmen! A drink for the gentleman!

BROWN: No, I really have to go——

RILEY: My dear fellow, let's put this business behind us for a while. I'm a family man myself.

CARMEN (*having reappeared*): What's going on?

RILEY: That's Carmen, the barman. One of the best. You can rely on his discretion. And my friend Able.

BROWN: How do you do?

RILEY: Bitter—I believe that's your drink. Would you be so kind, Able?

BROWN: Well, I——

(ABLE *goes for it.*)

RILEY: Relax. Don't worry. We're civilized people when all's said and done.

ABLE (*at bar*): Pint of bitter.

CARMEN: What's he doing?

ABLE: I don't know.

RILEY (*to* BROWN): You can trust me. I'm just an ordinary man like yourself. I know you're only doing your job—it's a dirty business, but when it's all over we're still people, aren't we? The world goes on. I expect you're sick of it all—life on the run—always looking over your shoulder, waiting for the knock on the door, the unguarded word, the endless lies, loss of identity—it's no life at all. You want to get back to your wife and your rose garden and live like other men—I know——

BROWN: Yes, I——

(ABLE *arrives with the beer.*)

RILEY: Ah! I expect you could use a drink.

BROWN: Just a quick one, then. You're very kind. Well—cheers! (RILEY *has placed the beer on the table between them. As* BROWN *reaches for it,* RILEY *slides it out of his reach and keeps his hand over it.*)

RILEY (*levelly*): Where's the tape-recorder?

BROWN: I——

25

RILEY: Just be sensible and we'll let you sleep—drink—anything you like. Just tell us.

CARMEN: Here——

RILEY (*sharply*): Give me that tape.

BROWN: I haven't got one!

RILEY: My patience is not inexhaustible!

CARMEN: Now then, Mr. Riley——

BROWN: I really don't know anything about tape-recorders.

RILEY: Ah!—well, you're talking to a man who does!

(*He has lost himself.* ABLE *remains loyal but bewildered;* BROWN *is just bewildered.*)

As a matter of fact, I've been experimenting with one or another of my inventions. I have a tape-recorder connected to my grandfather clock!

ABLE: What for?

RILEY: What for? What for? When Edison invented his lighthouse was he surrounded by a lot of peasants asking What for?

ABLE: I don't know, Mr. Riley.

RILEY: Well then! What exactly are you getting at?

ABLE: Nothing, Mr. Riley. I don't mean anything.

RILEY: It's a very cunning idea, that clock—it appeals to British character, bound to. It's a reminder of our glorious past— twice a day, noon and midnight—Rule Britannia!— And we need it— Did I go through the war to witness the decline of Britain as a maritime power? Did I sail the seven seas for that?

ABLE: I'm sorry, Mr. Riley.

BROWN (*unexpectedly*): Edison didn't invent the lighthouse, you know. You probably got mixed up with Eddystone.

RILEY: What?

BROWN (*bashfully half-singing, smiling hopefully, explaining*): My-father-was-the-keeper-of-the-Eddystone-light-and-he-met-a-mermaid-one-fine-night. . . .

(*A terrible silence.*)

RILEY: Your father was what?

BROWN: Not my father.

RILEY: Whose father?

26

ABLE: You can bet it wasn't a real mermaid.

RILEY: Shut up. (*To* BROWN.) Whose father was a mermaid?

BROWN: He wasn't a mermaid. He *met* a mermaid.

RILEY: Who did?

BROWN: This man's father.

RILEY: Which man's father?

BROWN (*testily*): I don't know.

RILEY: I don't believe you, Jones.

BROWN: Brown.

RILEY: This is just sailors' talk, the mythology of the seas.
There are no such things as mermaids. I'm surprised at a
grown man like you believing all that superstitious rubbish.
What your father saw was a sea lion.

BROWN: My father didn't see a sea lion!

RILEY (*topping him*): So it was your father!

BROWN: No——

ABLE: Why didn't you want to be a lighthouse keeper like him?
Too lonely?

BROWN: I didn't even know my father. (*Miserably.*)

RILEY: Ha! So it's just hearsay, is it? Not permissible evidence,
I'm afraid. (*To* CARMEN *who has been on the point of
interruption but held spellbound.*) My lord! I would
respectfully ask that the last line should be struck from the
record.

CARMEN (*weakly*): Mr. Riley——

RILEY: Now look here—I don't care if you name is Smith or
Jones or Robinson. I don't care if your father was a
mermaid or a sea lion or even your father. The question
is—*what are you playing at*?

CARMEN: Mr. Riley, I'll ask you——

RILEY: Silence in the public gallery! Now for the last time—and
remember you're on oath—I ask you in all solemnity—and
think carefully before you reply—I ask you—God dammit,
now I've forgotten the question—I wish you'd all keep
quiet!

BROWN (*moving out*): I've nothing more to say.

RILEY: Very well! Your witness!

ABLE (*entering into the spirit*): No questions, your honour!

27

RILEY: Stand down!

(*But* BROWN *has already scuttled out.*)

CARMEN (*suddenly furious*): I'm not going to have any more of that tomfoolery in here!

(RILEY *seems to be coming out of a trance. He looks round in bewilderment.*)

RILEY: What was all that about?

CARMEN: I said I'm not going to have any more of that! If you don't like it you can go somewhere else. Both of you.

ABLE: What did I do?

RILEY: What's the matter, Carmen? You ought to side with your loyal customers. Where would you be without them?

CARMEN: And I'm not sure that I wouldn't rather not either.

RILEY: You're not sure that you wouldn't rather not either? What's that supposed to mean?

ABLE: He means he'd rather have him than us but he's not sure. Either.

(*He sits down at his table and picks up his letter and scans it gloomily.*)

RILEY: I see. I see. Well, tomorrow I will be gone.

ABLE (*with letter*): It won't do, will it? . . . I wish I was a man of experience——

RILEY: I'll tell you quite frankly that there have been times when I've wondered if perhaps I've left it too late— wondered even if perhaps I didn't have it in me . . . till now . . .

(FLORENCE *has entered; bright, pretty, warm. She has been hurrying. She looks round but is disappointed, and goes to the bar.* ABLE *sees her.* RILEY *doesn't yet.*)

. . . till now. . . . Look at me and say, George Riley is on his way.

ABLE: I've seen blokes pick up a girl in twenty seconds. Afterwards I couldn't remember how they did it.

CARMEN (*to* FLORENCE): You missed him.

FLORENCE: Oh.

CARMEN: Harry.

FLORENCE: Yes.

CARMEN: Went to the races. Ten minutes ago.

FLORENCE: I might have known he wouldn't wait.

CARMEN: He had to catch the one-thirty.

FLORENCE: I couldn't find the place.

CARMEN: He said the same time tomorrow.

FLORENCE: He'll be lucky. (*Pause.*) Is that what he said?

CARMEN: Same time tomorrow.

FLORENCE: I'll have a drink on that then.

    (ABLE *has approached nervously.*)

ABLE (*strangled*): Allow me. . . . Would you allow me——

FLORENCE: Oh, what a lovely boy! Are you a Sea Scout?

    (ABLE *swallows dumbly.*)

ABLE: No . . . no.

FLORENCE: Gin and orange, thank you.

ABLE: Gin and orange.

CARMEN: Gin and orange.

    (*A heavy pause while* CARMEN *gets it and* ABLE *is crushed.*)

FLORENCE (*to* ABLE): Hello!

ABLE: Oh—hello.

FLORENCE: Hello. (*Smiles.*)

ABLE: Er, I've never seen you before in here.

FLORENCE: No. I just came to meet a friend.

ABLE (*rejected*): Oh.

    (*Pause.*)

FLORENCE: I just missed him. He left.

ABLE: Oh, him. Funny bloke?

FLORENCE: Funny?

ABLE: Oh, no offence.

    (CARMEN *with two glasses of gin and orange.*)

CARMEN: Five and eight.

    (ABLE *pays and gives glass to* FLORENCE.)

FLORENCE: Ta.

ABLE: Cheers.

    (*They drink. Pause.*)

    Did he ever tell you about his father?

FLORENCE: No, what about him?

ABLE: Well, I'm not sure, to tell you the truth.

    (*Pause.* ABLE *has lost confidence.* RILEY *gets up.*)

FLORENCE (*to* ABLE): The Navy's not what it was, is it?

RILEY (*approaching, grandiloquently*): Took the very words out of my mouth! Ah, we had a navy once! And we didn't take any lip from anyone. Now it's all down to committee meetings, points of order, general insolence and two or three obsolete aircraft carriers coming home backwards. George Riley.

FLORENCE: Florence . . . Lawrence.

RILEY: Flo-rence Law-rence . . . Flooorence Laaawrence! Poetry! (*Kisses her hand.*) This is Able.

FLORENCE: Like Cain and Abel?

RILEY: No, not at all. Like able seaman.

FLORENCE: And is he?

RILEY: Not noticeably.

ABLE (*progressively embarrassed, blushing*): My name is——

RILEY: He thinks you're a woman of exceptional beauty.

ABLE: I never——

FLORENCE: I think he's denying it.

ABLE: No.

RILEY: A bit inexperienced.

FLORENCE: No?

RILEY: Shy.

FLORENCE: I'm shy, too. (*To* ABLE.) Don't you worry.

ABLE: She came to meet that chap.

RILEY: Robinson.

FLORENCE: Who?

ABLE: His name wasn't Robinson.

RILEY: I remember, yes. Something about his father, wasn't it? Have you ever met his father?

FLORENCE: No, I don't think he's ever mentioned him.

RILEY: He lives in a lighthouse. Odd fellow.

FLORENCE: I think he was having you on.

RILEY: Never trusted him. And I'm an expert on human nature. I study it.

ABLE: I was thinking of going to the pictures tonight.

RILEY: Miss Lawrence, may I call you Florence?

FLORENCE: I think you'd better.

RILEY: Florence, I think you have a sensitive nature.

FLORENCE: Well, thank you, Mr. Riley.

RILEY: George.

FLORENCE: George.

ABLE: If you're not doing anything, I——

RILEY: I think you will understand.

FLORENCE: I beg your pardon?

RILEY: I've left my wife.

CARMEN: Now, Mr. Riley.

RILEY: I want you to know. Left her. Walked out. You married?

CARMEN: Mr. Riley——

RILEY: A man can take so much. After all, what is the home and hearth but an anchor?

FLORENCE: You're right there.

RILEY: The chain you have to drag along— You what?

FLORENCE: I said you're right. I could have been a dancer.

RILEY: You do know what I mean?

FLORENCE: Well, of course—it ties you down, doesn't it?

RILEY: Intelligence!

FLORENCE: Proper dancing. But my dad was sick. I was asked— an exotic tour——

RILEY: Intelligence in one so fair!

FLORENCE: Oh yes, I could have been dancing all over South America. It only happens once. Did you see a film called "Harem Nights"?

RILEY: What?

FLORENCE: I was nearly in that.

ABLE: Have you seen "The Sound of Music"?

FLORENCE: You wern't in that, were you?

ABLE: What? No. . . . No, I was wondering whether you would like——

RILEY: Able, do not think me rude——

ABLE: Oh, I don't think you're rude, Mr. Riley——

RILEY: But Florence and I have to talk. . . .

(*He leads her reluctantly to* ABLE'*s empty table and sets a chair for her.*)

Florence, you've never been to South America?

FLORENCE: No, my Dad was sick.

RILEY: I never have either. I mean that is one of the billion

31

things I have never done.

FLORENCE: Too late now.

RILEY: No—that's just it!

FLORENCE: Well, I think it is. (*She sits.*)

RILEY: It's the same for me. And I'm a cerebral man, Florence, I think, therefore I am!

FLORENCE (*warily*): Am what?

RILEY: What? I'm an inventor!

FLORENCE: An inventor?

RILEY: I have that honour. We're a small band of brothers, you know, each working to our separate goal.

FLORENCE: Yes, I'm sure.

RILEY: It's unrewarding toil—you see, (*sitting beside her*) inventors are working in the dark, plunging into the unknown. After all, the whole point of being an inventor is that you are inventing something that has never been invented before, otherwise what's the point of inventing it?

FLORENCE: Yes, I can see that.

RILEY: You can—yes, I can see you can. Florence, it's so rare to find someone who understands.

FLORENCE: Oh go on. There's lots of people that understand.

RILEY: No! There is no one. And now you.

FLORENCE: Well. . . . Well, how are you getting on?

RILEY: Florence, look at me. You see a man standing on the brink of great things. Below me, a vast flat plain stretches like an ocean, waiting to receive my footprints, footprints that will never be erased, and in years to come, people will see this once uncharted untrod path and say . . . George Riley walked this way——

FLORENCE: I don't know what you mean, Mr. Riley.

RILEY: Florence, you and I—we've been wasted. It has taken me years to make the break because I have always been alone. . . . But for you, Florence, it need not be like that, if there is someone beside you. Florence, I am . . . old . . . (*he looks at her carefully but there is no contradiction*) . . . no longer handsome, features that are perhaps more interesting than beautiful. . . . (*Pause.*)

FLORENCE: I should think you were quite good-looking when

you were young.

RILEY: I was, I was! Technically, I have made the break. (*He rises and strides away from table.*) I shall go back this evening, I suppose—well just to gather a few things, and tomorrow will see me in this spot. I'm meeting my partner —I have a partner, you know. There'll be a few details to settle and then the sky's the limit. And now you, whom destiny has cast in this shabby place at this golden moment —in you I see a fellow spirit.

FLORENCE (*getting up*): Well, that's nice. Thank you, George. And now I've got——

RILEY: Come with us, Florence!

FLORENCE: Go with you?—where to?

RILEY: Anywhere! Away! A new life!

FLORENCE: Oh, Mr. Riley, now——

RILEY: Florence, have you given up? What about South America? Uraguay—Paraguay— What about Peru?

FLORENCE: Yes, but honestly, Mr. Riley——

RILEY: You don't like me?

FLORENCE: Oh, I do. I think you're nice. I thought you were a bit loony at first, if you don't mind my saying, but you talk so lovely and I'm sure you're a very nice man, but . . . you don't even know me—— (*Crosses to bar.*)

RILEY: I do! Tonight you will go home and look around and see your whole life bounded by four flower-patterned walls, and you will cry Enough!—and you will come here tomorrow where I will be waiting for you.

FLORENCE: Really, Mr. Riley—you mustn't run away—otherwise it's all wasted, isn't it? Years . . . you can't throw away years——

RILEY: But I *have* been throwing them away— My life is piled up between me and the sun, as real and hopeless as a pile of broken furniture. Thirty years ago I was a young man ready to leave the ground and fly. Thirty years. . . . More, perhaps much more than the time I have left, and when a man's past outweighs his future, then he's a man standing in his own shadow. . . . Don't hesitate, Florence. . . . Do you trust me?

FLORENCE: Well, of course I *trust* you, Mr. Riley, but—why
don't you go back and give it another go—try once more.
(*Sadly.*) Don't you like your home?

RILEY: It's not a question of liking or disliking, it's what it does
to you . . . it's *nothing*, absolutely nothing. I give nothing,
I gain nothing, it is nothing. . . . My wife and I and Linda,
we get up in the morning and the water is cold . . . fried
bread and sausage and tea . . . the steam in the kitchen
and the smell of it all and the springs are broken in my
chair. . . . Linda goes to sell things . . . in Woolworth's . . .
cosmetics and toilet things, and we wash up when the
kettle boils again . . . and I go to my room . . . and sit
there . . . with my pencils and my workbench. . . .
(RILEY *moves away to the centre table and leans against it. A
spotlight picks him up and holds him there while the lights on
the bar slowly fade out, leaving him alone.*)
I've got a workbench, you know . . . and sit there. . . .
The Hoover is on H.P., Linda got it, she pays for it every
Friday and it drones all morning . . . like an aeroplane in
the house but far away . . . flying from room to room far
away, and the doors open and close so many times . . .
we've only got seven doors, but they open and close all the
time. . . . She always asks me, my wife, "Well, how're you
getting on?" she says, and I say, "Oh, it's coming, it's
coming. . . ." The way she says it, so . . . politely . . .
"How're you getting on?" . . . "Oh, it's coming, it's
coming." . . . I like to come in here for an hour or two,
have a drink, see what's about. Not many in here over
lunch, but it's people, you know . . . 'course I always go
home later, I've got to, you see, because of my work, and
she says, "What, still hard at it?" . . . and Linda is home
and there's chattering and cooking and eating again. . . . I
don't know what they're talking about half the time, the
wireless going because Linda wants it and she paid for
it . . . everything goes so quickly and the jokes on the
wireless aren't funny. . . . And then my wife says "Well!"
. . . "Well!" . . . and that means they want to go to bed.
Sometimes she says, "Well! Time I was in bed!" or "Well!

Time I was popping off!" Doesn't seem much point in
doing anything else, really. In the morning we get up and
the water's cold. . . . Nobody minds much. . . . She
doesn't. It wouldn't occur to her.
(*During this speech the bar set has faded out.* ABLE, HARRY,
CARMEN *and* FLORENCE *have already gone. The lights now
start to come up on the home.*)
She's used to it. She's got used to everything. She's even
got used to me. I don't surprise her any more—she's even
got used to me, whatever I do. And I do *do* things, which
ought to be surprising—like this idea of mine I'd rigged up
for watering the flowers—I mean it was something—
(PERSEPHONE *enters with two water-jugs, starts to water the
plants.*)
. . . and when I came down this morning, there she was,
just watering the flowers from a jug, as usual. . . . That
was the first thing that happens this morning. . . . (*To*
PERSEPHONE.) There's no need——

PERSEPHONE: Good morning, dear. . . . You're up late.

RILEY: There's no need, I tell you—I've put that water-jug out
of date—and a million others like it!

PERSEPHONE: George, I must ask you to take away all these
pipes and things. You've got your own room for your
experiments.

RILEY: Well! And I was down here till ten o'clock fixing it up
for you!

PERSEPHONE: Please, George, I'm not having the place looking
like a ship's engine room.

RILEY: At least give it a fair trial—wait until it rains.

PERSEPHONE: I'd rather water the plants with a jug.

RILEY: Married to a creative spirit, and for all you care I might
as well have stayed in my father's office.

PERSEPHONE: Well, if you had done you'd have a nice little
business now.

RILEY: It's scarcely believable. I thought there was supposed to
be an admiring woman behind every great man—an
ambitious wife. And you talk to me of offices! (*He stands
up angrily.*)

35

PERSEPHONE: Now don't get excited, George.

RILEY: How can I help being excited! For centuries while the balance of nature has kept flower gardens thriving with alternate sun and rain in the proportions that flowers understand, indoor plants have withered and died on a million cream-painted window-sills, attended by haphazard housewives bearing arbitrary jugs of water. For centuries. Until one day, a man noticing the tobacco-coloured leaves of a dessicated cyclamen, said to himself, what the world needs is indoor rain. Indoor rain of the volume and duration of natural rain. He considered: if for instance, one put a delicately poised sponge on the roof of a house, then that sponge would absorb rain and become heavy. Its density would increase, and density plus gravity creates energy. In short, the sponge would be just heavy enough to operate a valve, thus allowing the water system of the house to flow through prepared ducts, (*he demonstrates at the pipes*) and sprinkle itself wherever a flower is positioned. First Watt and the steam engine—now Riley and the Sponge Principle!

(*During this speech* PERSEPHONE *takes the water-jugs to the kitchen. She returns with Hoover which she plugs into the wall.*)

And that's not the end of it! What about this one!
(*Producing his envelope.*)

(PERSEPHONE *turns on Hoover and sweeps carpet.*)

(*Shouting over Hoover noise.*) It came to me lying in bed— take a look at it—the sheer audacity of such a conception——

PERSEPHONE: No need to shout, George.

RILEY: You push that damned machine round as if I'm talking about the weather.

PERSEPHONE: Well, you were talking about the weather, weren't you? I'm just trying to get on with my work. (*She vacuums round the sofa, he has to move one foot.*) Move your foot. (*He moves his foot.*)

RILEY (*shouting*): I was not talking about the weather. I was talking about my new envelope.

PERSEPHONE: Well, I hope I'm not stopping you.

RILEY: I'm telling you about my invention and you keep buzzing that stupid machine.

PERSEPHONE: Oh, very well, dear. I'm sorry. (*She switches off Hoover. Looks at him.*) Now, what was it again?

RILEY: It came to me in a flash—just this morning. I'm home.

PERSEPHONE: Of course you are.

RILEY: I mean home and dry. I can't see any snags. (*Waving the bigger envelope.*) It's all here!

PERSEPHONE: It's quite small, isn't it?

RILEY: Some of the biggest things in our line are very small to look at. Think, there's the match.

PERSEPHONE: A match?

RILEY: Yes.

PERSEPHONE: What kind of match?

RILEY: Eh? No, no—what I've done is the *envelope*.

PERSEPHONE: An envelope for matches?

RILEY: Who's talking about matches?

PERSEPHONE: You were, love.

RILEY: No, I damn well wasn't!

PERSEPHONE: As you like, George. Now, I really must get on.

RILEY: No, wait a minute. Here, look. (*He takes his envelope out of the bigger one, gives it to her.*) Absolutely new, never been done before.

(PERSEPHONE *takes it, glances perfunctorily and makes to hand it back.*)

PERSEPHONE: Very nice, I'm sure.

RILEY: You haven't noticed.

(*She turns it over.*)

You see? Gum on both sides.

PERSEPHONE: So it has. (*Returns it.*) So it has.

RILEY: Pretty cunning, eh?

PERSEPHONE: Gum on both sides. Whatever will you think of next?

RILEY: So you can use it twice.

PERSEPHONE: Twice! . . . How do you get it back after you've posted it the first time?

(RILEY *discouraged. Silence.*)

RILEY: It's about time Linda was home. It's Saturday, you know.

PERSEPHONE: Don't worry yourself. She never forgets, does she?

RILEY (*irritated*): I didn't mean that. I just wish she would come. Nice to *see* her. (*Pause.*) How much is she earning now?

(*Hoover on again.*)

PERSEPHONE: Now, we've been into all that before. We get along very nicely.

RILEY: You know, that girl isn't using her potential, that's the trouble. A girl like her, serving in a shop.

PERSEPHONE: She's in charge of Fancy Goods now. Have you been in? The other girl on the Fancy Goods sort of works under her.

RILEY: Fancy goods! It's still serving in a *shop*, isn't it? That's no kind of a job for a daughter of mine. She's got brains. She must have. She's *bright*. She should be above that—she should be a secretary—a *private* secretary. I mean, how can she be content with that, a girl like her. She's got no . . . *drive*—she doesn't make any *effort* to better herself.

PERSEPHONE: Well, she hasn't had the training has she? She makes enough to keep us going.

RILEY: Yes, but— (*Lamely.*) She isn't using her potential, that's all I'm trying to say.

(PERSEPHONE *turns off Hoover and coils up flex.*)

It's not that I don't *appreciate* (*pause*) . . . You can't make much at inventing, not at first. It's not that sort of job. It's been such a fight. Such a chancy business, inventing.

PERSEPHONE (*without a trace of sarcasm*): Very chancy, I should say.

RILEY: It is, it is. It's the markets, you see. It's a case of winning the markets with something that really catches the imagination. I think I'm on to something here. Funny thing is, I don't feel any different. You'd think you'd *feel* different, somehow. I feel just the same.

PERSEPHONE: But you feel all right?

RILEY: Of course I feel all right. It's just that you should feel . . . *different*. I never knew anyone in this house who didn't

38

feel just the same as always, whatever. You've got to get outside to feel anything at all.

PERSEPHONE: It's very hot outside today, boiling. But summer is always the best season, I always say. It's the warmest. Very warm today, *very* warm. I don't know.

RILEY: It's nothing to do with the weather.

PERSEPHONE: I thought salad for lunch, don't you? It's cooler on a warm day like this. I got a bit of lettuce and there's a tin of meat.

RILEY: I don't know what you're talking about.

PERSEPHONE: Well, it's no mystery, dear. Salad is best for a hot day.

RILEY: What if it is?

PERSEPHONE: It's so warm, I just thought salad would be a good idea.

RILEY: Don't you ever *listen*?

PERSEPHONE: Well, of course, dear. Don't fret yourself.

RILEY: Don't fret yourself, don't worry yourself . . . you don't have to go on as if I'm neurotic. I'm just trying to tell you things.

PERSEPHONE: Please, George, I must get on.

(PERSEPHONE *carries Hoover off and upstairs.* RILEY *follows her upstairs, talking as he goes.*)

RILEY: She's got to use her potential, that's all I meant. Otherwise you're wasting yourself, aren't you? She doesn't care. Serving in a shop. Mixing with goodness knows who. Who was she with last night?

PERSEPHONE: Same one.

RILEY: I don't approve of him.

PERSEPHONE: You've never seen him.

RILEY: He's a *motor-cyclist*, isn't he? You never saw a *gentleman* on a motor-cycle. She's aiming beneath herself all the time.

(PERSEPHONE *dusts banisters.*)

PERSEPHONE: She'll be down in a minute. Don't start her off.

RILEY (*brooding*): Who'd have thought a daughter of mine would go around with a motor-cyclist. I didn't bring her up like that. (*Catching up.*) What do you mean "down"?

39

PERSEPHONE: Downstairs. (*Returning downstairs.*)

RILEY: Well, isn't she at work? (*Following her down.*)

PERSEPHONE: No, she's in her room.

RILEY: What's she doing in there?

PERSEPHONE: Having a lie-in, I suppose.

RILEY: Having a *lie-in*? You mean she's been up there all this time?

PERSEPHONE: She didn't come in till late.

RILEY: Well! It's not good enough. She can't lie in bed all hours. It's a lazy habit.

PERSEPHONE: She didn't come in till late. (*Exit to kitchen.*)

(*But* RILEY *is already shouting from the doorway.*)

RILEY: Linda.

(*From upstairs, a cheerful* "*Hello!*")

What are you doing there at this hour?

LINDA (*off*): What do you think?

(*This almost defeats* RILEY, *but he returns to the attack.*)

RILEY: It's nearly twelve o'clock!

(LINDA'*s reply is laconically bellowed.*)

LINDA (*off*): Thanks!

(RILEY *gives up.* PERSEPHONE *returns to room, dusts.*)

RILEY: She shouldn't do it, you know. You shouldn't let her. When I was her age——

PERSEPHONE: Now please don't have a row first thing. I can't face it, I didn't get a wink of sleep last night.

RILEY: I heard you snoring through the wall.

PERSEPHONE: That clock woke me up. You'll have to take it down.

RILEY: I will not. My work is the one thing I will not have interfered with. Just because I invented it and it works you resent it.

PERSEPHONE: I resented it last night all right.

RILEY (*he is at the door, looks up the stairs and turns back*): And that girl. Where does she get it from? (*Wisely.*) She's a very incomplete person, you know. . . . She's a mess.

(*From upstairs an unintelligible bellow from* LINDA.)

(*Angrily.*) Stop yelling round the house. Come down here and speak properly. (*To* PERSEPHONE.) That's her, isn't it?

She thinks she owns the place. No regard.

(*Sound of* LINDA *thumping downstairs.*)

She's impulsive—selfish—and—*loud*, she's so loud. . . . I can't understand it.

LINDA (*enters, without greeting*): I said—what happened to my sponge?

(*She moves swiftly into the kitchen and back.*)

RILEY: This isn't a hotel, you know.

LINDA: You're telling me. (*Sags into settee.*) Is there any tea?

PERSEPHONE (*going out to get it*): It's nearly dinner.

RILEY: What are you doing in bed till lunch time?

LINDA: Playing the pianner.

RILEY: Well, in future, you don't traipse downstairs at any time you feel like in your pyjamas.

LINDA: Right.

RILEY: You will appear dressed and tidy.

LINDA: Right.

RILEY: Lie-abeds never get anywhere in life.

LINDA: A lot of people get up at dawn and never get anywhere in life. (*Pointedly.*) Or half past eight for that matter.

RILEY: I've done a whole morning's work while you've been in bed. And I was up late fixing things. Not that you're ever about to see. What time did you get in last night?

LINDA: I don't know. I was carried home unconscious from an orgy.

RILEY: You haven't even noticed.

LINDA: What?

RILEY: And what's more, I've come up with something only this morning that's going to change the whole——

(LINDA *groans.*)

I've come up with a winner!

LINDA: So have I!

RILEY: What?

LINDA (*jumps up gaily*): A winnah! Oooooh, he's love-ly, he's my fair-y prrince! He's my knight in sil-ver arm-our!

RILEY (*sourly*): He's a motor-cyclist.

LINDA (*hamming it up in tremendous spirits now*): He's my *sheek*! He's dark and handsome and love-lay!

41

RILEY: He's common.

LINDA: He isn't common—he's *unique*. He's me unique sheek!

RILEY: Where do you meet these people?

LINDA (*breathlessly*): *We-ell*, I was in the desert one day, you
see, and all of a sudden, before I knew *where* I was, I
heard the thunder of horsepower and a strong brown arm
*scooped* me up and as we roared into the sunset he
co-vered me with burn-ing kiss-es and put me on his
pillion! (*She has almost choreographed this. She stops soberly
in mid pose—soberly.*) I met him over the Fancy Goods. He
kept turning up. I was beginning to think he was a nut on
fancy goods. But he wasn't. He fancied me. (*Pause; shout.*)
Is there any tea?

(*She notices the pipes, follows the piping with her eyes in
wonder.*)

What in God's name is all this?

RILEY: If you didn't stay out all night and in bed half the day
you'd know all about it.

LINDA: What the world needs is a lot of amateur plumbing in
every living-room.

RILEY: It's only the prototype.

LINDA: What of—an oil refinery?

RILEY: It's an extension of natural rain for indoor plants. They
will be watered just as the flowers in the garden are
watered. When it rains outside, these plants will receive the
same volume of water over the same duration of time. It's
all connected to the water supply, you see. Think of the
saving in labour, it's a most ingenious invention.

(LINDA *studies the ceiling thoughtfully.*)

LINDA: You could have made a hole in the roof. . . .

(*She collapses once more into settee and like a dying voice in
the Sahara calls.*)

Tea! For pity's sake give me tea. . . .

(*Pause.*)

RILEY: I used to read to you.

LINDA: What?

RILEY: You're never about, are you?

LINDA: About where?

42

RILEY: Here, I never see you.

LINDA: Well, you see me now.

RILEY: What do you want to do then?

LINDA: Like what?

RILEY: Well, what should we do? We can—go walking in the park, for instance.

LINDA (*genuinely puzzled*): What for?

RILEY: What do you mean, what for? You don't have to have a *reason*. We never had a reason before.

LINDA: Before when?

RILEY: Before when we used to go walking in the park!

LINDA: Eh? Well, for God's sake, I was twelve years old! Anyway, I want to brush my hair this afternoon and get ready.

RILEY: Get ready for what?

LINDA: For tonight, of course.

RILEY: Again? You went out last night.

LINDA: And I'm going out tonight. And I'm going out tomorrow night. What's up with you today?
(*Pause.*)

RILEY: How long's this one going to last? Couple of weeks? (*Pause.*) Well, don't say I didn't warn you.

LINDA (*barely controlled*): Warn me about what?

RILEY: You never learn, do you?

LINDA: Never learn *what*?

RILEY: Always rushing in over your head.

LINDA: *Rushing in over my head?*

RILEY: Headlong. Out of your depth. You think each moment's going to last forever and then you're brought down with a bump. You never learn.

LINDA: Dear God. . . .

RILEY: Watch where you're going. Take stock. Test the ground. Don't jump in with your eyes shut. That's the way you get hurt.

LINDA: Thank you.

RILEY: No constancy, that's the trouble. One boy after another, each one going to last for ever. I've seen it happen. You're living in a fool's paradise. You build them all up and at

43

the end of it it's just another pimply boy moving on to someone else.

LINDA: Oh, shut up.

(*Pause.*)

RILEY: What do you do when you go out?

LINDA: Talk.

RILEY: What about?

LINDA: What do you mean, what about? (*Shouts.*) Mu-um, isn't that tea coming—I'm dying!

RILEY (*heatedly*): The way you behave in this house! Anyone would think you were the head of the family or something. I never bawl orders around like that and I *am* the head of the family.

LINDA: So I notice.

RILEY (*angry*): Well, it's about *time* you noticed! Just remember it. You act as if I don't exist. What about this lout on a motor-cycle—I've never even set eyes on him. You never asked me, did you?—my approval. No. Well, just start remembering I'm your father.

LINDA: So what?

RILEY: So what? I'll tell you so what. You're going to bring that young man here and introduce him properly for my approval.

LINDA: Like Bernard.

RILEY: There you are you see—another flash in the pan.

LINDA: I don't know what you're talking about half the time. You made a right idiot of yourself with Bernard Morrison and you made me look pretty stupid too.

RILEY: You let yourself in for that—telling me he was going to take you on a cruise on his family's shipping line.

LINDA (*heatedly*): I told you his father worked on a boat.

RILEY: Don't blame me if he went off you. I was only doing what any father would have done.

LINDA: You told him I was your only treasure and you hoped he'd cherish me in the years to come.

RILEY: What's wrong with that?

LINDA (*furiously*): He only came round to take me to the pictures!

44

RILEY (*equally furious*): Well, how was I to know?

LINDA: And you're not supposed to ask people if they've got any hereditary diseases in their family. He must have thought you were barmy.

RILEY (*more furious*): How dare you talk to me like that! And as for this motor-cycle hooligan, you're going to bring him round here and then you may go out with my permission and you're going to be home every night at eleven o'clock. What's his occupation?

LINDA: At least he's got one—that reminds me— (*Goes out and upstairs.*)

RILEY (*calling upstairs*): Why did they give you the morning off?

LINDA: They didn't. I couldn't face them today, that's all.

(RILEY *is genuinely appalled by this.*)

RILEY: What! You've never done that before.

LINDA: Well, I did today, didn't I?

RILEY: They'll give you the sack.

LINDA: Don't be silly. I'll go in on Monday and tell them I wasn't well. What's the matter with you? (*Goes off upstairs and returns down with handbag.*)

RILEY: What's the matter with me? I'm disgusted, that's what's the matter with me. It's disgusting. That's no way to get on in your work—*malingering*. Lying in bed because you can't be bothered to go to work. I'm ashamed of you, Linda. I'd never have thought a daughter of mine would waste herself like that. That's the last time you miss work—you hear that? You owe a responsibility to your work—and to yourself—you——

(*During* RILEY'*s speech* LINDA *has brought on her handbag. Out of it she takes a red zipped purse and out of the purse a ten-shilling note, which she now hands him, cutting his speech off dead.*)

LINDA: Here you are, another ten bob down the drain. Seems a funny thing giving your own father pocket money. Specially when he never gave you any. (*Shouts.*) Ma! Are you bringing the *tea*!

RILEY (*deflated*): Now Lindy—that's not fair—you know you'll get it all back.

45

(*He produces a small notebook and pencil and writes in it.*
LINDA *slumps down on to the settee.*)

. . . Saturday, July the fifth. Ten shillings, that brings it up
to seventy-two pounds, seven and six. That's for the week
when you were a bit short. You only gave me seven and
six. Remember?

LINDA: Don't remind me.

(PERSEPHONE *enters with tray of tea for one which she sets on
table behind sofa. There are two cushions on the settee, one
behind* LINDA. PERSEPHONE *looks round the room critically,
then approaches the unused cushion, straightens it, fluffs it up,
pats it.*)

PERSEPHONE: Get up a minute.

LINDA (*indicating the Queen on the wall*): If she's coming I
should put her picture straight.

(LINDA *moves over and sits back against the cushion*
PERSEPHONE *has just tidied.* PERSEPHONE *tidies the other
cushion, pats it.* LINDA *moves back. The first cushion is back
in its original state. She kneels on the second cushion and
pours herself a cup of tec. But* PERSEPHONE *has gone to the
wall to straighten the Queen.* LINDA *shakes her head and
lolls back in the settee.*)

RILEY: Lindy, Lindy—your faith is about to be rewarded!
Look—it's all here—there's a fortune in this envelope!
(PERSEPHONE *exits to kitchen.*)

LINDA: You've got money in there? Where'd you get it from?

RILEY: It's not exactly money, not yet. . . .

LINDA: Oh, I see. What is it?

RILEY: An envelope.

LINDA: I can see that. What's inside it?

RILEY: Another envelope.

LINDA: Dead clever. And what's inside that?

RILEY: Eh? Nothing.

LINDA: It can't fail. Honestly, I don't see why you can't get
money from the Labour Exchange. It's just silly—it's
sitting there waiting for you.

RILEY: Let's not have that again. I told you—that's for the
unemployed people. You've got to be out of work.

46

LINDA: When were you ever in it?

RILEY: Linda, it's for people who haven't got a job!

LINDA: Oh dear. . . . Well, how long am I supposed to be handing out to you every week, that's all I want to know. Putting it down in that silly little book—what's it supposed to *mean*? I wouldn't mind giving it to you so much if only you wouldn't keep writing it down in that bloody book.

RILEY: Don't talk to me like that! How dare you talk to me like that?

LINDA: Whose money is it anyway? And where does it go? Beer every dinner-time until you've spent it and then wait until next Saturday.

RILEY: Don't talk to me! I said don't talk to me!

(PERSEPHONE *enters with a cup and saucer, plate of biscuits.*)

PERSEPHONE: For goodness sake, what's going on? You've upset him— You shouldn't upset yourself, dear.

RILEY: My envelope's going to get me out of all this.

(PERSEPHONE *pours herself a cup of tea.*)

PERSEPHONE: That's right, dear.

RILEY: Of course it is, it's the law of averages.

PERSEPHONE: Of course it is, you tell them.

RILEY: Tell them what?

PERSEPHONE: Whatever you think is right, dear.

RILEY: Tell who?

PERSEPHONE: How should I know, dear? You're the inventor.

RILEY: That's right—I'm the inventor.

LINDA: What's he ever invented?

RILEY: A lot of things!

(PERSEPHONE *pats* LINDA'*s cushion.*)

Dozens, dammit.

(PERSEPHONE *finds a book stuffed down the side of the sofa. Holds it up.* LINDA *falls back on the tidied cushion.*)

PERSEPHONE: Hullo, what's this doing down here? Rupert Bear. . . .

(*She holds it up, a big coloured children's book.*)

RILEY: It's one of Linda's. From when she was little.

PERSEPHONE: I know that, dear.

LINDA: He was reading it.

RILEY (*heatedly*): I was not!

PERSEPHONE: Well, it doesn't matter.

LINDA: He was reading it. I saw him. Not that I want it, thanks. Far as I'm concerned he can read it as much as he likes. (*Scornfully.*) Fairies——

RILEY (*explosion*): I wasn't reading it! . . . I was looking at it. There's no law against it, is there?

PERSEPHONE: Of course there's not. Why shouldn't he read it if he wants to?

RILEY: I wasn't——

LINDA: I just think it's soppy, that's all. Rupert.

RILEY: It's a book, isn't it? When did you last read a book?

LINDA: I've read seven books in my life and they were all dirty.

PERSEPHONE: Linda!

RILEY: You see?

LINDA: What?

RILEY: No culture. No culture in young people nowadays. How can you expect to make something of yourself?

LINDA: Like you, I suppose.

RILEY: Yes, like me. I was given a mind and I use it. I don't go through life as if it was a public escalator with nothing to do but watch the swimsuits go by.

LINDA (*getting up*): How can he go on like that? Ever since I remember he's been going up to that damn room. What does he do it for? Why doesn't he just sit downstairs and stop pretending? It used to be so nice . . . once . . . at that crummy school. . . . "What does *your* dad do?" . . . "My dad's an inventor." Most of their dads were just bus conductors and milkmen and labourers and mechanics. Some of them didn't have jobs at all. But my dad was an inventor! . . . Amazing how long it took me to see through that! I must have been thick. So what am I supposed to do now, join in the game? Well, I don't think I'm going to play much longer. I'm not enjoying it.

PERSEPHONE: Now, Linda!

LINDA: Sometimes the girls at work ask me what you do. Want to know what I tell them? "Nothing!—Nothing at all!"

RILEY: No——

LINDA: I tell them, "My dad's out of work!"

RILEY: Lindy——

LINDA: "He hasn't got a job!" What I don't tell them is that you're too stupid to collect your unemployment money. I don't mind you not having a job—I wouldn't be the first girl there with an unemployed father. But I'm damned if I'm going to be the first with a lunatic as one!

RILEY: Lindy! . . . You shouldn't go on like that . . . it's going to be different—it's changing now. I've been unlucky before, but I've got a new idea now and there's nothing that can go wrong with it. It's the simplest idea I've ever had. That's where I've been going wrong before, I've been aiming too high—at complicated things, expensive things sometimes. The clock, for instance—oh, it's good in its way, very good, but it's a luxury, the market's too specialized. I've been going at the wrong end of the scale, I can see that now. . . . Here, look—look now—I want to show it to you—both of you—here——

PERSEPHONE: I've seen it, dear.

RILEY: I want to explain about it. You see, this envelope——

LINDA: —Plays God Save The Queen.

(*Pause.*)

RILEY (*quietly: momentum gone*): I don't like this house.

PERSEPHONE: Linda, don't be rude to your father.

LINDA: Yes mam.

RILEY (*louder*): I don't like this house.

PERSEPHONE: An envelope for matches, was it, George? Go on then, tell us about it.

RILEY (*very loud*): I don't like this house! (*Silence—quietly.*) I'm leaving.

PERSEPHONE: Now, don't get excited, love. Why don't you go along to the Arms for a quiet drink while I get the dinner. You can go to the pictures afterwards. You like going to the pictures on Saturday.

RILEY (*standing*): I'm leaving.

LINDA (*quietly*): And I'm not coming back.

RILEY: And don't take it for granted I'm coming back.

PERSEPHONE: No, all right, dear, you just pop along and——

RILEY: Didn't you hear me?

LINDA: We heard you.

RILEY: There is nothing to stop me going away for good now——

LINDA: Every Saturday I give him his pocket money and he runs away from home——

PERSEPHONE: Not every Saturday.

RILEY: Why don't you believe me?

PERSEPHONE: Now, George, who said I didn't? (*Stacking tea things.*)

RILEY: There are things a man can do—and a man will always do the unexpected when he is driven to it. I don't even feel guilty about it—do you realize that? I've been held back enough—too much—why should I feel guilty?

PERSEPHONE: I don't know, dear. Why?

RILEY: Why? You're not following me. I said I *shouldn't*.

PERSEPHONE: Shouldn't what?

RILEY: Feel guilty about it.

PERSEPHONE: About what?

RILEY: About not coming back.

LINDA: Aren't you coming back then?

RILEY: No! As of now, no.

PERSEPHONE: You mustn't mind Linda— After all, she does support us. (*Exit to kitchen with tea-tray.*)

RILEY: Well, she won't have to support *me* any more. And don't worry, she'll get her money back. There's enough in this envelope idea to take care of that and a hundred times more. (*To* LINDA.) I don't want you to think that your little loans haven't been appreciated. Because they have. You'll get it back—the first thing I'm going to do is send it to you.

LINDA: Can I have it in fivers?

RILEY: All right, so you shall. In fivers.

LINDA: Thanks.

(*Pause.*)

RILEY (*uncomfortably*): Well, I'm sorry it's got to end like this. It is not what I would have wished. I know I have not been a model husband and father, but I have done my best

50

in difficult circumstances, and I cannot get on unless I get out.

(*Turns to go out of the door but his exit is spoiled by* PERSEPHONE *returning with a shirt to mend.*)

So let us not have any long drawn out farewells, I shall simply go. Well—good-bye, everybody.

(PERSEPHONE *is busy at work-basket.*)

PERSEPHONE: Good-bye, dear, don't be late.

RILEY (*explodes*): For God's sake, I'm not coming back!

PERSEPHONE: All right, no need to shout, George. I didn't mean anything.

RILEY: I'm not going to stop till I'm right up there! It only needs one small idea that I can take with me—something to keep me on my feet when I step over the side——

LINDA (*quietly*): This boat isn't everything.

RILEY: This boat isn't the whole world, you know. It's all over there!

LINDA: Aye aye, captain.

RILEY: Don't you worry—I'll reach it.

(LINDA *has been sitting spent, dead-voiced, now she gets up and goes to him straightfaced.*)

LINDA: We shall miss you, father, but I'm sure it's for the best. God bless you and all who sail in you.

(RILEY *leaves; the grandfather clock whirrs and starts to chime Rule Britannia.* LINDA *sits heavily and closes her eyes.*)

I think I'll go mad . . . I've already got a twitch.

(*The music ends.*)

PERSEPHONE: You shouldn't have missed work today. It's not fair on the other girls.

LINDA: They shouldn't make us work Saturdays. No one else does.

PERSEPHONE: Nearly everybody does. I work Sundays.

LINDA: No one I know. Janice Pringle works four and a half days and gets two pounds more.

PERSEPHONE: You should change, then, shouldn't you? You've got to have a bit of gumption if you want to get on. (*Takes button and thread to table and sits, sewing button on shirt.*)

LINDA: She had the training.

PERSEPHONE: There you are—you should have stayed on at Commercial College, it pays in the end.

LINDA: She's a trained *masseuse*, at the health club——

PERSEPHONE (*blithely maintaining course*): *And* you could have got into the teachers' college. They said so. You had good chances.

LINDA (*roundly*): Janice Pringle says she could make a hundred pounds a week if she branched out on her own. . . .

PERSEPHONE: You see—you've got to push yourself. There's better jobs for you.

LINDA: Yes, I think I'll be a brain surgeon. . . .

PERSEPHONE: You had the brains to be a teacher. That would have been nice, with long holidays. . . .

LINDA: . . . I'll take a course of postal tuition. . . .

PERSEPHONE: But you wouldn't listen to me, would you?

LINDA: "A brain surgeon in six months. Astonish your friends."

PERSEPHONE: Nobody ever listens.

LINDA (*bitterly*): Janice Pringle wouldn't be astonished. . . . Janice Pringle says nothing would astonish her. . . .

PERSEPHONE: What do you keep going on about Janice Pringle for?

(LINDA *gets up, finds her bag, takes out wages envelope.*)

LINDA (*with the bogus excitement of the TV host*): Satter-day is here again.

(PERSEPHONE *accepts the money, puts it in her apron pocket.*)

PERSEPHONE: Thanks.

LINDA: Oh, I wish it was tonight. That's the one thing I can count on—I wake up and think—it's all right—it'll soon be tonight and I'll be off out and he loves me.

PERSEPHONE: Don't count your chickens.

LINDA: I know him.

PERSEPHONE: You always know them.

LINDA: I *know* him.

PERSEPHONE: You knew Bernard Morrison too, didn't you?

LINDA (*carelessly*): He's got engaged—did I tell you?

PERSEPHONE: Who has—Bernard?

LINDA: You'll never guess who to?

PERSEPHONE: Janice Pringle . . .?

LINDA (*found out*): Well, she's welcome. I can do better than that for myself.

PERSEPHONE: Fancy that.

LINDA: She came at me flashing this *invisible* diamond. I could have puked all over it.

PERSEPHONE: Time enough for you.

LINDA: I don't care anyway. (*Getting happy.*) I'm going to make myself look a knockout tonight—I'm going to wash my hair and do my nails and stick Blue Grass up my jumper!

PERSEPHONE: Linda! (*Pause.*) You like him as much as Bernard?

LINDA (*derisive*): Bernard!

PERSEPHONE: As much as that David, then?

LINDA: I didn't love *him*.

PERSEPHONE: What?—more than whatsisname—Brian?

LINDA: *Brian?* Honestly! (*Then she catches on.*) It's not like that, you know. It just isn't. They were *kids*.

PERSEPHONE: Well, you're a kid, aren't you?

LINDA: Well, I'm not going to be one for ever, am I?

PERSEPHONE: No, I suppose not.

LINDA: I mean, what happens then?

PERSEPHONE: I don't know.

LINDA: You can't count on a sudden wave of loony patriotism to put a Rule Britannia clock in every home.

PERSEPHONE: Well, don't worry about it.

LINDA: Don't worry about it. . . . Don't worry about it. I *do* worry about it.

PERSEPHONE (*putting sewing things away*): You'd better get dressed, Linda. We don't want another row when he gets in.

LINDA: He won't get back till late—meatless Saturday for George Riley, the man who's on his way . . . to the pub on the corner.

(*The lights start to come up slowly on the bar.*)

PERSEPHONE: Well, why shouldn't he go to the pub? At least he meets people.

LINDA: How do you know? I bet he's just another lonely feller having a quiet drink.

(CARMEN *enters from above bar to behind it.*)
The point is, what's he like? I mean when we can't see
him. He's got to be different—I mean you wouldn't even
know me if you could see me——
(ABLE *enters as before and crosses to centre table with letter.*
PERSEPHONE *goes off to kitchen.*)

PERSEPHONE (*leaving*): Come on, Linda.

LINDA: And that goes for everyone. There's two of everyone,
you see——
(BROWN *enters as before.*)
You need that
(HARRY *enters as before.*)
and if the two of him's the same, I mean if he's the same
in the pub as he is with us, then he's had it.
(RILEY *enters as before.*)

RILEY: Enter a free man!
(*Music;* "*Rule Britannia*" *starts and increases until the end of
the act.*)

LINDA: Poor old Dad. . . .

PERSEPHONE (*at door*): Linda! (*Goes upstairs.*)

LINDA (*following her off*): You'll have to do something about
him, you know. . . .

RILEY: Unashamed I have left her.
(*The lights on both sets start to fade out.*)

LINDA: Before I'm old and ugly.

RILEY: A good woman I daresay, in many ways a fine woman,
in many ways a terrible liability. . . .
(*The lights are out.*)

CURTAIN

END OF ACT ONE

## ACT TWO

*Before the curtain rises; "Rule Britannia".*
*The lights come up on the home.*
*The living-room. The next day. Late morning.* PERSEPHONE *is starting to lay the table.*

LINDA *bounces in jauntily, looking good in jeans and sweater. She is eating a slice of cake.*

LINDA: Morning.

PERSEPHONE: I don't know why you bother—I could have brought your dinner up on a tray.

LINDA: The concert woke me. Hello, I thought (*to the tune of "Rule Britannia"*) It's tw-elve o'clock, time-to-get-you-up, pom-pom—it's twe-e-e-e-e-e-lve o'clock!

PERSEPHONE: It woke *me* up last night.

LINDA: Yes, that'd be one of the snags when it came to shifting it in millions.
(*She snaps on the radio which is playing a "Family Favourite".*)

PERSEPHONE: Were you late last night?

LINDA: Yesss! I was so late last night I was earl-y this morning!
(*She choreographs round the room ending up with a kiss on* PERSEPHONE'*s head.*)
(PERSEPHONE *remains detached.*)

PERSEPHONE: Did you have a nice time?

LINDA: Yess! I did have a nice time. In fact I had a gorgeous time. And I'm going to have another gorgeous time tonight and ev-erynight!

PERSEPHONE: Turn it down a bit, will you? It's making my head ache.
(LINDA *turns down the radio.*)

LINDA: Is there any tea?

PERSEPHONE: Expect so. You won't want any breakfast now.

LINDA: I had lovely dreams. We were going to Gretna on the

55

motor-bike.

PERSEPHONE: I'll have the dinner ready in an hour.

LINDA: Do you ever think of yourself that there's a kind of sameness about your life?

PERSEPHONE: It'd be a funny life if there wasn't.

LINDA: My, you do hold your own, don't you? (*Roundly.*)

PERSEPHONE (*tolerant*): All right. Put the cutlery round for me, will you. (*She exits.*)

(LINDA *puts cutlery round.*)

(*Returning with side-plates.*) I can't see what he sees in you in those trousers. Specially on Sunday.

LINDA: What's Sunday got to do with it?

PERSEPHONE: Well, it's not very nice. Sunday. Church and everything.

LINDA: I always wondered where those people were going. Don't get much of an example in this house.

PERSEPHONE: I've got the dinner to see to. You'd be the first to complain if there was no hot dinner on a Sunday.

LINDA: Yes, I like my nosh.

PERSEPHONE: My boyfriends would've been ashamed to be seen with me if I'd gone out like that.

LINDA: You had boyfriends, then? Before you got married?

PERSEPHONE: Why? Do you think you invented them?

LINDA: Oh no. I should think you were smashing.

PERSEPHONE: Yes I was.

LINDA: Did you look like me?

PERSEPHONE: No.

LINDA: Oh.

PERSEPHONE: You look all right.

LINDA: Do you think so? It's my fingers that worry me. I worry quite a lot about my fingers. I mean, no one would take me for a *violinist*.

PERSEPHONE: You could have been a teacher, though.

LINDA: Do you ever think to yourself that . . . (*Abandons it. Examines her fingers.*) Yes, I've got a good idea for this television panel game. You get people to show their hands and the panel has to guess what they do. You can have mystery guests shoving their hands through two holes in a

56

screen. . . . (*Looks at her hands.*) Lady strangler. . . .

PERSEPHONE: Yes, I had suitors.

LINDA: Soootors!

PERSEPHONE: So don't be in such a hurry. I turned down one or two before your father.

LINDA: Did you? Were you ever sorry?

PERSEPHONE: What a thing to say!

LINDA: Well, were you?

PERSEPHONE: No. No, I wasn't. I knew he wasn't . . . safe, like most people are safe. But safety isn't everything. A safe man in a safe job. Well, it's not everything.

LINDA: It's money, though.

PERSEPHONE: There's lots of people like your father—different. Some make more money, because they're different. And some make none, because they're different. The difference is the thing, not the money.

LINDA: Well, that's nice, isn't it? What am I doing in a rotten shop? I could stay at home and be different. Starving but different. Terrific.

PERSEPHONE: You haven't got it in you.

(*Pause.*)

LINDA: I say——

PERSEPHONE: What?

LINDA: Did any of your—suitors—ask you to go away with them?

PERSEPHONE: Away where?

LINDA: Just away.

PERSEPHONE: You mean, elope?

LINDA: Yes, all right then.

PERSEPHONE: Certainly not.

LINDA: Would you have gone if they'd asked?

PERSEPHONE: I told you.

LINDA: Would you have thought it was romantic?

PERSEPHONE: What?

LINDA: Just—going away with a feller. On the spur of the moment. Would you think it was romantic?

PERSEPHONE: Plain stupid. (*Pause.*) What did you tell him?

LINDA (*jumps*): Who? (*Found out; collects herself.*) I said—

57

I couldn't.

PERSEPHONE: That's right.

LINDA: That's right. . . .

PERSEPHONE: If he's worth it, he'll wait.

LINDA: Suppose he won't.

PERSEPHONE: Then he's not worth it.

LINDA: It's not that simple, though, is it? I mean, if he was worth it and didn't wait, that wouldn't be exactly unbelievable. So what am *I* waiting for?

PERSEPHONE: You could wait for your twentieth birthday.

LINDA: I might be dead by then.

PERSEPHONE: Well, I might. (*Exit.*)

(*In the wait,* LINDA *comes to terms.* PERSEPHONE *comes back with dustpan.*)

LINDA: You better not.

PERSEPHONE: What?

(LINDA *turns it aside; moves, heaves, stops.*)

LINDA: There's going to be no end to it, is there? He'll never give up.

PERSEPHONE: Perhaps he will. (*Sweeping up* LINDA'*s crumbs.*)

LINDA: He won't. He's living in dreamland. . . . Where is he, anyway?

PERSEPHONE: Upstairs. Now don't set him off today.

LINDA: Why should I?

PERSEPHONE: I mean, if he says anything about leaving again. . . .

LINDA: Oh, he came back, didn't he? He always comes back.

PERSEPHONE: Yes, he came back. (*Hesitates.*) But—I don't know—he was behaving very off . . . excited; when he came back from the pub.

LINDA: Had a bit too much, I expect.

PERSEPHONE: Well, don't set him off. You know what he's like. (*Pause.*)

LINDA: What was he like before?

PERSEPHONE: Before when?

LINDA: I mean—when you—when he was young—was he always——?

PERSEPHONE: He was—proud. Oh yes, he would *create* . . .

58

something, anything.

LINDA: You shouldn't have let him leave the family business. It was at least a kind of security.

PERSEPHONE: I *made* him leave it.

LINDA (*incredulous*): You *believed* in him—in all *this*?

PERSEPHONE: The business was temporary for ten, eleven years. It would have been temporary all his life. If he was going to be a failure anyway, he was better off failing at something he wanted to succeed at. So he would be an inventor. It appealed to him. He liked to . . . break bounds. He got hold of a bit of enthusiasm. That was worth a lot.

LINDA: That was worth nothing! You had to work in a shop and now *I* work in a shop—and that's worth something.

PERSEPHONE: Just try to be charitable, Linda.

LINDA: *Try?* I *am* a charity, I work at it full-time— You and me, we're the Society for the Preservation of George Riley! God, if his father hadn't died, he wouldn't even have a house to live in!

PERSEPHONE: You want to know what he was like—? He was a gentleman. (*Pause.*) You'd better call him—and tell him to wash his hands. He usually forgets.

LINDA (*getting up*): Gentleman George. . . . (*At door.*) *Dad!* Well, I hope he's calmed down since yesterday. I don't like waiting for the balloon to pop in his face. It's bad for my nerves.

PERSEPHONE: I don't know what he wants to stay up there for working on a Sunday. He always likes to take a day off.

LINDA: A day off from what?

PERSEPHONE: You don't have to be unkind, you know.

LINDA: I'm not unkind. I mean I don't feel unkind. Funny thing is I'm more embarrassed than he is when he comes back from his little outings. I never know what to say.

PERSEPHONE: Well, don't say anything.

LINDA: That's worse—that's weird. It's *weird* pretending it never happened.

PERSEPHONE: Did you tell him to wash his hands?
(LINDA *turns and yells.*)

LINDA: And wash your hands!

If he was honest he'd come down and say, "I've decided that some people are cut out to make a living and some people are cut out to lie in bed, and I'm the bed type so I'll be upstairs if you want me and if you're not doing anything at four o'clock I'll have a cup of tea. . . . Two lumps." Instead of that, he sits up there doing damn all. It's a situation, isn't it?

PERSEPHONE: It occupies him.

LINDA: Oh, I'm sure it passes the time very nicely. But it's driving him half-barmy.

PERSEPHONE (*sharply*): Your father isn't barmy.

LINDA (*not in the least put out*): Half barmy. Well, you can't expect me to be sentimental about him. I mean, life hasn't been like a National Savings advert, has it? All the happy family round the fire and the ruddy spaniel chewing the slipper. (*Pause.*) Anyway, I don't mean he's mad or anything. If he was *Lord* Riley he'd be called eccentric. But he's just plain old George. So he's half barmy.

PERSEPHONE (*defiantly*): We've got on very well together in our way. I know plenty of women whose husbands have taken to drink or gambling or well—you-know-what, and it's not much comfort to say that at least they're all there in the head.

LINDA: He just hasn't grown up all over the same speed. He's getting worse and personally I don't think we're helping him by treating it all as normal.

PERSEPHONE: I know, it's very difficult. Without hurting him. You don't want to hurt him, do you?

LINDA: He's hurting himself in the long run.

PERSEPHONE (*unhappily*): Well, I don't know.

LINDA (*pause*): Shall I call him again?

PERSEPHONE: You'd better. Perhaps he dropped off. He had a very restless night.

(LINDA *goes to open the door.*)

I hope he's washed his hands.

(LINDA *gets to the door just as* RILEY *comes downstairs. He is wearing his best suit, clean shirt, tie. He carries in one arm a briefcase and drawing-board with a coat over his arm.*

*The other hand is holding a large battered suitcase. The effect is spoiled by carpet slippers.*)

LINDA: Oh no!

PERSEPHONE: Whatever is it?

LINDA: He's packed!

PERSEPHONE (*going to door*): He's what?

LINDA: I told you it'd get out of hand. He's got all his gear now.

PERSEPHONE: Oh, my goodness.

(RILEY *enters, puts his things down by the window and walks to the settee, next to which lie his shoes. During the first part of the scene he sits on the settee and is changing into his shoes.*)

RILEY: Don't let me interrupt you, I've only come for my shoes.

PERSEPHONE: What's all this then?

RILEY: Do I have to repeat everything? I told you last night— I'm leaving.

LINDA: Oh, Dad! Don't make a thing of it. We apologize. I apologize.

RILEY: Apologize? Nothing to apologize for.

PERSEPHONE (*calm*): Where're you thinking of going, dear?

RILEY: To meet my partner. I'm going into industry.

LINDA (*with a dangerous quietness*): You're going where?

RILEY: I'm going to develop my invention. I told you. My envelope. It's revolutionary.

LINDA: Oh—is it as revolutionary as that bottle-opener?

RILEY: What bottle-opener?

LINDA: That bottle-opener which would've revolutionized bottle-opening only no one had invented the kind of bottle-top your bottle-opener needed to open bottles.

RILEY (*a fractional pause*): This is an envelope. It's simpler than that.

LINDA: Simple, is it? You mean simpler than that pipe which would never go out as long as you smoked it upside down?

RILEY: It's simpler than that, too.

LINDA: Well, it's not as simple as you are.

PERSEPHONE: *Linda!* Be quiet!

LINDA: No, I won't!

61

RILEY: This isn't like the others—this is the real thing—you'll see.

LINDA: The only thing he's ever invented is a way of having a job without earning any money.

PERSEPHONE: Stop it, *please*.

LINDA: Listen, he's not going—he's not going this time.

RILEY (*accusingly*): The trouble is, you haven't got faith in me, have you?

LINDA: Faith!

RILEY: Well, you did once, didn't you?

LINDA: Faith? Faith in what?

RILEY: Faith in *me*! I used to tell you—yes I did—and you had *faith*—can't you *remember*—can't you remember it was happy?

LINDA: You dreamed it. How can I have faith in a bottle-opener?

RILEY: Before that, Lindy.

(*They are both nearly shouting.*)

In the park. We used to walk in the park, and don't deny it—*you had FAITH*!

LINDA: Oh *Jesus*!—stop living in my childhood. I was a *child*—and you were my *father*.

RILEY: I'm your father *now*.

LINDA: I was ten—eleven—I don't know—you know what he's got in his room—you know what *books* he's got?

PERSEPHONE: Oh, Lindy——

LINDA: Noddy, Mickey Mouse, Fairy Annual—all my old books I had when I was a kid—Rupert—he's got the blood-y *lot*!

RILEY: I'm going! (*And he makes the move.*)

(*It snaps off* LINDA's *hysteria, and she comes close and speaks with a strained gentleness.*)

LINDA: Listen, dad—father—you don't have to go this time. You really don't. You don't have to prove anything for us. Just stay and don't bother, don't worry about having to prove anything—will you?— Just stay and be like other people. Put that case back, and we'll have our dinner, and go for a walk if you like, and tomorrow I'll go to the Labour Exchange with you and you can register. It's only signing your name. And you'll get money, every week, if you just *register*, and maybe they'll find you something you really like, and you'll get more money, and if you *don't* like it you don't have to *do* it, and you *still* get money—it's the Government—it's all there—official, do you see? Please? (RILEY *has listened patiently, and a little amused. He speaks to her with equal gentleness and the same air of explaining to a small child.*)

RILEY: No, listen, Lindy, you don't understand—this isn't *like* the other times—I've got to go because I promised—I've arranged to meet my partner, you see—this time it's all laid on—it's *definite*. This man is impressed, you see, and we're going to *manufacture*, we're going to have a factory to *produce* envelopes—he's putting the money up, you see—this time it's *real*.

LINDA: Dad, you don't have to—dad, you're making it up— you *know* you are—you don't have to——

RILEY (*almost jubilant, but still quiet*): I'm not! It's all *true*!

LINDA (*nearly crying*): Dad, you *dreamed* it.

RILEY: No-o-o! You'll see—I'm not *alone* this time— Oh Lindy, I'll come back in a Rolls Royce and then you'll believe me again and it'll be happy again.

LINDA: Dad, it'll be happy now if you stay and tomorrow we'll go to the——

RILEY: You don't understand—I don't need it now.

PERSEPHONE (*a plea*): Oh, let him go.

LINDA (*losing her gentleness now*): Dad, if you go this time, I swear, I promise, you won't get any more pocket-money— ever—if you don't register I'm not going to give it to you, for your own good as well as ours—I swear it, if you don't stay home, now.

RILEY: I'll pay it all back, Linda, you know that.

LINDA: You don't *have* to pay it back.

RILEY: But I *will*. I *want* to. It'll be easy. Seventy pounds is nothing to what I'll be worth soon.

LINDA: Dad, you're not going to be worth anything, ever. You'll come back tonight, like always, and—what's the *point*?

PERSEPHONE: Let him go.

LINDA: No—it's gone too far.

RILEY: Why don't you believe me?

PERSEPHONE: It's better for him, Linda.

(LINDA *breaks*.)

LINDA: *But what about me?* (*Then quieter*.) What about me?
There's no end to it—and I've *waited*. I've waited for it to
change but it's not going to, is it? I'm stuck. I'm stuck here
in this tidy little house waiting for it to change so I can get
out. Well, I'm not going to any more—because I've been
*asked*. Yes, I have. He loves me and I've been asked.

PERSEPHONE: Oh, Linda——

LINDA (*turning on her*): So he's different! Well, *I'm* not different
—I just want to get married and get on with my own life.
'Cos he asked me to go away—north—he asked me——

RILEY: What?

LINDA: Yes he did. Well, I'm going, mum—I can't wait till your
old age pension—I can't wait ten years! Because I've had
my go, and it's not fair. It's not fair. (*She is near tears*.)
(RILEY *approaches her*.)

RILEY: Marry? You?

LINDA: Yes, me!

RILEY: What—to that motor-cyclist? You can't, not yet.

LINDA: Why not?

RILEY: Because I haven't given my permission, that's why not.
I'm your father! And I don't suppose he's got any
intention of marrying you.

LINDA: Yes he has!

RILEY: He never said so, did he?

LINDA: Yes he did!

RILEY (*they are both shouting each other down*): Look at me—he
never said marriage, did he?

LINDA: I don't care if he didn't!

RILEY (*draws breath*): The ingratitude! Is that how I brought
you up?

LINDA: You never brought me up at all.

RILEY: I took you for walks!

LINDA: Oh Jesus Christ, we should have got him a dog!

RILEY: I don't even know his name! And I'm your father! That's what's gone wrong here—no respect. That's why I'm being driven out—you ask me why—well, that's why—because here I don't exist! And now you want to run away with some young good-for-nothing. You've only just left school!

LINDA (*dully, on her way out*): Three years, dad. A hundred and fifty ten bobs. Don't you remember? Seventy-two pounds, seven-and-six. That's for the week I was short. (*Exit.*)

(PERSEPHONE *has stood quiet; almost grieving.*)

RILEY: She'll be back, you know. It's all in her head.

(PERSEPHONE *sits down.*)

Oh, I didn't want to leave her like that, though. (*Pause.*) She used to be so . . . nice. (*Pause.*) She'll be back.

PERSEPHONE: Yes, perhaps.

RILEY: I've got to go.

PERSEPHONE: Go where, George?

RILEY (*a bit thrown by her*): . . . I met this man in a pub, you see——

PERSEPHONE: You met a man in a pub.

RILEY: He's my partner. I can't let him down.

PERSEPHONE: Oh, *George*— She means it, you know.

RILEY: He's counting on me.

PERSEPHONE: I don't blame her.

RILEY: You see, we're going to make our own. Produce them.

PERSEPHONE: Oh—please!

(*Pause;* RILEY *uncomfortable.*)

George——

RILEY: I have to go now.

PERSEPHONE: Give it up—I'm asking you.

RILEY: Now? At a time like this——?

PERSEPHONE: I'll help you——

RILEY: You don't understand—it's all starting now.

PERSEPHONE: Where? What are you going for?

RILEY (*high*): I told you!

PERSEPHONE (*giving up*): All right.

RILEY (*sympathetically*): I have to.

PERSEPHONE: All right. (*She turns away.*)

65

(RILEY *picks up his bag and pauses.*)

RILEY: Look, there's something else. I didn't want to say anything in front of Linda.

PERSEPHONE: What do you mean?

RILEY: I don't want to keep anything from you. I want to be fair.

PERSEPHONE: You're always fair, George.

RILEY: Well, there's this other woman.

PERSEPHONE: I beg your pardon, George?

RILEY: Another woman.

PERSEPHONE: Which other woman?

RILEY: What? You don't know her.

PERSEPHONE: Who?

RILEY: The other woman, dammit—you know.

PERSEPHONE: Oh, I see.

RILEY: Yes.

PERSEPHONE: Since when?

RILEY: Since yesterday.

PERSEPHONE: Since yesterday.

RILEY: I met her in the pub.

PERSEPHONE: Did you?

RILEY: She knows what I'm trying to do, you see. We have this understanding.

PERSEPHONE: What understanding?

RILEY: Spiritual you could call it.

PERSEPHONE: Spiritual.

RILEY: I just thought you ought to know. (*Pause.*) Well . . . I'll be writing, I expect.

PERSEPHONE: Don't get too warm carrying all that stuff. It's really hot again today. Perhaps you can leave your coat at home.

RILEY: I'll be needing it later. The weather will change.

PERSEPHONE: Of course, there is that. Good-bye, then. . . .

RILEY: It was a long time ago. (*He looks round, and leaves.*)

(LINDA *appears in the doorway, looking exhausted.*)

LINDA: I mean it.

PERSEPHONE: I know.

LINDA: I've been asked and I'm going. Today.

PERSEPHONE : Going where?

LINDA : I don't know— Up north . . . I don't care. (*Pause, stronger.*) It's the best thing—for him too, I mean.

PERSEPHONE : Perhaps.

LINDA (*a hesitancy*): You'll be all right, the two of you. Won't you . . .?

PERSEPHONE : Are you asking or telling?

LINDA (*stronger*): What I mean is, when I'm gone he'll *have* to do something about it—won't he?

PERSEPHONE : Will he?

LINDA (*up*): Can't you see?—I'm keeping it all going! I've got to get out, Ma!

(*Pause. She misunderstands* PERSEPHONE'*s troubled reserve, her withdrawal. Gently;*)

I'll be all right.

(PERSEPHONE *picks up tray and gathers the plates and cutlery on to it.*)

PERSEPHONE (*coldly, almost cuttingly*): Well that's fine, then, isn't it?

LINDA (*reacting up*): Well what am I supposed to *do*? There's just no end to it. We're carrying him, you and me, and I don't know about you, but I'm tired. He may be a lovely feller to stand a drink in the pub, great value for money, I'm sure—but as the family joke he's wearing a bit thin. We're lumbered, and we'll go on being lumbered till he's dead, and that may be *years*— (*She catches herself, contrite.*) Oh God—I didn't mean that—I just meant——

PERSEPHONE (*angry*): You didn't mean anything because you don't know anything and you don't think. You don't ask yourself why—you don't ask yourself what it costs him to keep his belief in himself—to come back each time and start again—and it's worth keeping, it's the last thing he's got—but you don't know and you don't think and you don't ask. It costs him—every time he comes back he loses a little face and he's lost a lot of face—to you he's lost all of it. You treat him like a crank lodger we've got living upstairs who reads fairy tales and probably wishes he lived in one, but he's ours and we're his, and don't you ever talk

67

about him like that again. (*Spent.*) You can call him the family joke, but it's our family. (*Pause.*) We're still a family.

LINDA (*unrepentant but briefly subdued; not sarcastic*): Rule Britannia. . . . Well look at it this way— When he goes off with my ten bob in his pocket either he knows it's all a sham, in which case the whole thing's a game at our expense and he knows it—or, he really thinks he's going, in which case he's walking out on us and the best of luck. Either way the family doesn't mean so much to *him*.

PERSEPHONE (*tersely*): All right—you just go——

LINDA (*up*): Well I'm right, aren't I? You're just taking the easy way and making it sound like love. You let it start and you haven't got the guts or the common sense to stop it. It's crazy! You're not helping him, so who are you helping? He's got worse and worse and your whole bleeding life is a waste of time, and you don't care about anything except tidying up the mess. What's the *point*? What are you being tidy *for*?

PERSEPHONE (*quietly*): I've kept our life tidy—I've looked after you, and him, and got you this far—perhaps it is a waste of time. You never went to sleep on a damp sheet and you never went to school without a cooked breakfast—and what was the point of that? I worked for you—I stood behind a counter so that your school clothes were the same colour as everyone else's. What was the point? You tell me why I worked late for a red blazer. It hasn't all gone your way, but it's a good home—you've never wanted for a kind word and when you looked for a clean hanky or a jumper you found it. What was the point of that?

LINDA (*subdued, blankly*): The only girl in our class with her old green blazer was Alice Maynard. We made her life hell. (*Looks up at* PERSEPHONE.) I'm sorry. When all's said, I'm going because I love him and I'm afraid if I don't go I'll lose him. That's all. (*Pause.*) Look, I'm not going to Australia.

(PERSEPHONE *moves, breaking the mood.*)

PERSEPHONE: You can't take much on a motor-bike.

68

LINDA (*smiles wanly*): I'll leave me furs and just take me
    jewellery. (*Pause.*) And my radio—I want my radio——
    (*Holds it.*)
PERSEPHONE: Well, it's yours.
LINDA: It's the first real thing I bought—and no one else
    listens to it——
PERSEPHONE: It's yours to take.
LINDA: Yes. (*She turns it on and hugs it. It plays softly. She goes
    to the door. Joylessly.*) I'll write.
    (*She goes out. After a moment* PERSEPHONE *takes up the
    tray and follows.*)
    (*The home fades out and the bar comes up.*)
    CARMEN *enters to behind the bar, and* ABLE *to beside it. They
    look at a newspaper.*)
    (*RILEY enters. He does not enter dramatically, but with great
    significance: he has a big suitcase, briefcase, drawing-board
    and a hat and coat. He makes a point of finding a safe and
    ostentatious place for his "things"— He is complacent, aware
    of the effect he is achieving on* CARMEN, *who stares at him
    dubiously.* RILEY's *triumph is quiet but deeply and excitedly
    felt. He is playing it down, but his smile reveals the import.
    He has acquired a bunch of flowers.*)
CARMEN (*indicating the case, etc.*): What's that?
RILEY (*carelessly*): My things. Am I the first to arrive?
CARMEN: What?
RILEY: Harry not in yet, I take it.
CARMEN: Not yet.
RILEY: And Florence.
CARMEN: Who?
RILEY: Florence. The girl from yesterday.
CARMEN: Oh. She said she was coming in.
RILEY: Of course she's coming in. She's coming to meet me.
    (*To* ABLE.) Been here all night?
ABLE: No. Just got in.
CARMEN: What's going on, then? (*The cases again.*)
RILEY: Big day. What will you have?
ABLE: No, you have one with me, Mr. Riley.
RILEY: Yes, I'm a man to keep in with. Thank you. Half and

half.

ABLE: And the same again for me, Carmen——

CARMEN: My name's not Carmen.

ABLE: I wondered if it was.

CARMEN: Well, it isn't.

ABLE: What is it then? Carmen's a girl's name, isn't it? (*He goes to the bar and pays.*)

(RILEY *is sitting at the table.*)

RILEY: His name's Victor, but it doesn't rhyme with barman.

ABLE: Victor, not a bad name.

RILEY: Doesn't rhyme with anything.

(*Pause.*)

ABLE: My name's not Able. (*He comes over with the drinks.*)

RILEY: My name's not Ethelred.

ABLE: Ethel's a girl's name, too.

RILEY: Or Charles.

ABLE: Do people call you Charles?

RILEY: No. It isn't Richard, either.

(*Pause.*)

ABLE: My name's Richard.

RILEY: So it is.

ABLE: Dick. Stupid name, but people always say that, don't they?

RILEY: Nothing much wrong with Dick. Good English name. Three kings of England have been called Dick. By their friends.

ABLE: What'd you call me Able for?

RILEY: Doesn't rhyme with seaman.

(ABLE *has been trying but losing all the time. With this he bows to greater genius and gives up.*)

ABLE: Well, cheers!

(*They drink.*)

How did she take it?

RILEY: Who?

ABLE: Perse—whatshername.

RILEY: Persephone.

ABLE: That's a funny name. I don't know anybody called that.

RILEY: Nor do I.

ABLE: Except her.

RILEY: Her name's Constance.

ABLE: Why d'you call her Persephone? Doesn't rhyme with anything.

RILEY: I didn't know anyone called Persephone. I thought I ought to.

ABLE: Did she mind?

(*Pause.*)

RILEY: She never knew.

ABLE: It's a funny life.

(*Pause.*)

RILEY: She didn't take it very well, now you ask.

ABLE: I didn't mean to poke my nose in——

RILEY: Not well at all. She wept of course. And Linda, Linda was upset—well you see she didn't understand. I won't deny it depressed me a little. Now that I've done it. After all those years, you're bound to leave something behind. Still, you can't go on with it. Not for ever.

ABLE: I suppose so.

RILEY: They'll be all right. . . . My daughter got engaged today.

ABLE: Oh. Congratulations. Nice feller?

RILEY: Very nice. He's a motor-cycle manufacturer.

ABLE: What's his name—Norton?

RILEY: Yes.

ABLE: Caw! Well, she'll be well looked after, then.

RILEY: Oh yes—he's doing very well.

ABLE: I should say so. When's the wedding?

RILEY: Not fixed yet. Of course, that's going to leave quite a gap in the family. She was very close to her mother.

ABLE: Ah.

RILEY: Yes. I'm a bit worried to tell you the truth. I mean— she'll be all alone now.

ABLE: Who?

RILEY: My wife. She'll be all alone.

ABLE: Oh.

RILEY: I mean—what's she going to *do*? I didn't know about Linda, you see. Mind you, she'll be better off without me, I think. And I'll be supporting her, of course.

71

ABLE: She'll be all right, then.

RILEY: Oh yes. Yes she will. To tell you the truth, I don't think I'm an easy person to live with.

ABLE: No?

RILEY: No. Not an easy person altogether.
(*Pause.*)

ABLE: Mr. Riley. . . . About that girl, Florence. . . . I mean, what do you think she thought, really?

RILEY: Oh, she *understood*. Yes, no doubt about that——

ABLE: Do you really think she'll come. . . .

RILEY: Of course she'll come, no need to worry about that.

ABLE: I don't know how you did it. I mean, I know she seemed quite struck by you . . . quite interested—but I never would have thought . . . just like that——

RILEY: What's the matter with you?

ABLE: Nothing's the matter with me. I was just wondering whether she might change her mind—have second thoughts or something.

RILEY: Why should she?

ABLE (*thoughtfully*): It's fantastic. . . . I don't know how you did it. (*Gloomily.*) I'll never get my turn, I know that.

RILEY (*stands up*): Where is everyone? (*Pause.*) You know, I think Harry and I will make a team all right. He's a simple fellow, crude you might almost say, but he's got the . . . dash for it, good raw material. You see he needs me just as much as I need him. Separately we're tied down, but together we—what's the word?

ABLE: Click?

RILEY: Thank you—complement each other. The world's full of Harrys. People who'll never get anywhere until someone gives them the impetus. They've got ideas of getting on, but not the whole means, some vital elements missing. They try to make it up with a loud mouth, but they never get far. . . . It's self-deceiving. They need that steadying influence of a more thoughtful nature . . . that's the combination to success. Ingenuity plus industry. He's got his little capital but not the . . . intellect to use it to advantage. I'll be able to get him on all right. . . . We should have quite a little business going in time if things go well. Quite a little business.

ABLE: Well, if there's any man can do it, it's you, Mr. Riley.

RILEY: And there'll be branching out, too, of course, because I'll be working on other ideas at the same time.

ABLE: It all sounds great, Mr. Riley. . . . Think Harry will turn out all right? Bit of a sharp one, if I'm not mistaken.

RILEY: Oh, I can handle Harry, I'm used to handling men. If you ever feel you've had enough of the Navy, Able, I'm sure I'll be able to find a place for you in the organization. Get in on the ground floor, you know, that's the rule in business. Grow with it, you see. We'll be big business one day . . . our name will mean something. . . . *Riley and* . . (*Pause.*) . . . Hey, what's Harry's other name?

ABLE: Search me. Don't think I'll be leaving the Navy for a bit though. Suits me fair enough. 'Course you can't really tell after only a few months but it gets you around, you know. . . .

RILEY: Yes, that's the great thing.

ABLE: And there's a few perks, too. As a matter of fact I feel a bit lost on leave. . . .

RILEY: Florence and Harry shouldn't be long now.

ABLE: How long are you going to give them?

RILEY: How d'you mean? They'll be here in a minute.
(CARMEN, *really out of boredom, comes over to get the empties.*)

ABLE: I'm surprised you make a living, Vic.

RILEY: Who?

ABLE: Carmen. I'm surprised you make a living.

CARMEN: I don't.

RILEY: Well, I don't mind helping the poor if they keep their place. We'll have the same again.

ABLE: No, my privilege, as they say. It's the last time, don't forget.

RILEY: You shouldn't spend your money.

ABLE: Nothing else to spend. Smoke? (*Proffering.*)

RILEY: Oh well, thank you, Able. You know, I've never set foot outside the country. That's a terrible thing really—I mean,

73

to be born into the world and to have only one chance to be in it and *still* only see one tiny bit—it's hardly believable that anyone would take so much on trust, when you think about it. If we were each born into a separate room and had to stay in it, by the time we died we'd know every corner of it. But the world we take on trust. How do I know that Japan really exists? Or Tahiti. Or America or Morocco or—or *Manchester*? I've only got another people's word for it. How could I have let it happen?

ABLE: Were you an "objector"?

RILEY: What?

ABLE: Why didn't you go abroad in the war?— Were you an objector?

RILEY: Yes. Well, no. Not really. Not at all. I designed things. I was in a special place, I designed—bombs, special inventions for war. I stayed in this big house, in the country, where they couldn't bomb us.

ABLE: You were important—one of the backroom boys.

RILEY: Oh yes. I invented a water-cooled machine-gun. Well, what it was—I *adapted* a water-cooled machine-gun so the soldiers could make tea in it while it was firing.

ABLE: Tea?

RILEY: It boiled the water.

ABLE: That's clever.

RILEY: Oh, I sent them a lot of ideas like that. Sent them to the War Office. . . . They never replied.

ABLE: No?

RILEY: No. Well, there was a war on. . . . (*Pause.*) . . . Hong Kong . . . colours, the colour of it all. Chinese junks and palms. . . . Aden! Naples! But how do I know they are really there? For all I know, it is possible, it is just possible, that nothing else exists, or if it does, then in some fantastic form which, by an elaborate conspiracy, has been kept secret from me. . . . And all the maps and newspapers and photographs which suggest the existence of China and Africa are all part of a gigantic hoax. . . . My, Able, if I'd had your opportunities! You're a travelling man, Able. You *know*—you have *seen*. . . .

ABLE: I've only done one foreign trip so far. . . . I suppose it's all right, yeah.

(*Pause.*)

RILEY: Odd thing is . . . I sometimes think of myself as a sailor, in a way . . . with home as a little boat, anchored in the middle of a big calm sea, never going anywhere, just sitting, far from land, life, everything. . . .

ABLE: Well, you're on your way now, aren't you?

RILEY: Oh yes . . . yes, I'm on my way all right. Me and Harry. We'll have some decisions today. We'll have to find a little place to rent, see about a machine . . . paper, glue. . . . Oh, there'll be a lot of things to do in the first days. I wish he'd come. And Florence. Where've they got to? . . . Oh, I can't wait to get started, I feel . . . inspired. Being in at the birth, that's the great thing. Watch it grow, all yours. It'll mean work, of course, I've no illusions about that, but it's worth it when you're doing it for yourself, seeing it happen. . . . Bigger and bigger. . . . Envelopes pouring out of the machine . . . a whole row of machines . . . a factory . . . we'll have a sign—Big electric letters against the sky—*Riley and*——

(*The climax drops. In the pause,* FLORENCE *enters.* RILEY *goes to her elated.*)

Florence! I knew you'd come—I knew it. Didn't I tell you—Able?

FLORENCE: Oh hello, Mr. Riley——

RILEY: George!— You're here at last— Where are your things?

FLORENCE: Things?

RILEY: Did you bring anything with you? Oh but, I knew you'd come—my partner will be along—you'll like him—we're all in this together——

(*She looks nervously at* CARMEN.)

CARMEN: Yes, well . . . who's drinking, then— Have a drink and then Harry will turn up and——

RILEY: Of course! Champagne! Put it on my account!

CARMEN: You haven't got an account and I haven't got any champagne.

RILEY: You haven't? Why not?

75

CARMEN: Well, there's not much call for it.

RILEY: Dear me, of course there's no call for it if you haven't got it. You don't know the first thing about business, Carmen.

FLORENCE: Well, it's all right, I don't want any champagne anyhow——

CARMEN: Gin and orange?

FLORENCE: Thanks a lot. (*To* ABLE.) Hello.

ABLE: I was just wondering if——

RILEY: Wait! (*He goes for the flowers.*)

(*The door is flung open and it is* HARRY, *in a great rush.*)

FLORENCE: Harry!

HARRY (*excited and breathless*): Hell-ello, hello, hello, hello! How's my little stripper, then? Never answer the phone, do you? Kept you waiting, have I?— Serves you right for yesterday. Now then—

(*They hug while* HARRY *natters greeting and affection.* RILEY *is standing, looking at them, dazed. He doesn't move and does not say anything.* ABLE *is looking on open-mouthed.*)

(*Talking fast.*) Hey, listen—we've got to be moving, we're going to make a day of it and there's a train we've got to be on so no time for chat. (*To* CARMEN *facetiously.*) Nothing today!

FLORENCE: Yes, yes—oh lovely. Where're we going? The sea?

HARRY: Near the sea. Epsom.

FLORENCE: Hey, there's no racing on Sunday!

HARRY: Got to see a man about a horse.

FLORENCE: Oh, Harry! Don't you know anybody except horses?

HARRY: Of course I do. There's some of the boys waiting for us at the station so we better beat it. Don't worry—it'll be a lot of fun, you'll love it, you'll see.

FLORENCE: Oh Gawd, I thought at least on Sunday I'd be free from horses.

(HARRY *suddenly becomes aware of* RILEY *and particularly the flowers. He senses something of the situation, though not much, and this is* HARRY *the comic.*)

HARRY: Hello then! What's this? Flowers? Not flowers for my little doll? (*Stricken.*) How could I be so blind! Behind my

back! How long has this been—so it has come to— (*To* FLORENCE.) Where have I failed you, my dah-ling? (*Snapping out of it.*) Haaah! Come on then! (*He makes to leave.*)
(RILEY *has been frozen, now he seems to be moving out of a trance.*)

RILEY: Harry! Where're you going? What about us?

HARRY: What about us?

RILEY: Our plans! (*Desperate.*) My envelope—your envelope—God, you remember——

HARRY: Oh, God, are we still on that? Listen, George—I mean—look—show. (*He gestures for the envelope.*) Show . . envelope.
(*Very slowly, unwillingly,* RILEY *brings out the envelope which he puts into* HARRY'S *impatient hand.*)
Right—now watch me. You write me a letter (*he mimes it*) and you seal it up (*he licks it and seals it*) and you post it (*mime*) and the postman gives it to me (*mime*) and I open it (*he rips it open across the top*) and then there's this gum on the other side of the flap, so I . . . (*He tails off, having explained enough. He holds up the envelope, ripped, unusable, ridiculously so.*) With it? The flaw in the ointment, as they say. Never mind, back to the drawing-board—keep trying, there's always something else—what about a cup with no handle for people with no hands—Keep trying— All right?
(RILEY *is staring at him.* HARRY *crumples up the envelope and tosses it on the ground.*)

FLORENCE (*sensing part of it, too*): Mr. Riley——

HARRY: Christ, come *on*! Or we'll miss it. (*He pulls her by the hand.*) Cheers. (*To* CARMEN.) I'll stop by for one next time—come on then—we'll miss that——
(HARRY *and* FLORENCE *go out in an untidy rush.* RILEY *stands still.* CARMEN *is still embarrassed.* ABLE *is recovering from his own awaking.*)
(*Silence.*)
(RILEY *speaks with evident effort to sustain dignity.*)

RILEY: Ah yes, yes. . . . Yes, I think he's got a point, you know. How very extraordinary. (*Turning to* CARMEN *who is in*

*sympathetic attendance.*) The fact is, it was not a very
*practical* idea, though it did have a certain . . . flair. . . .

CARMEN: Oh yes, Mr. Riley, it had a lot of flair.

RILEY: But not practical.

CARMEN: A bit impractical, yes. Ahead of its time.

RILEY: Is that it?—is that it? Yes—well, of course the public
isn't ready—that's true, they go around ripping envelopes
to shreds. . . .

CARMEN: That's just about it, Mr. Riley.

RILEY (*going to door and gathering up his things*): Quite. Well,
never mind, never mind—I've got a few shots left in my
locker, oh my goodness yes—let's see there's my, er . . .
my . . .

(ABLE's *laugh starts coming through loud and clear.*)

ABLE (*laughing*): You didn't even know his name. . . .

(RILEY *is hurt to anguish, turns and leaves.*)

(*The lights fade on the bar.*)

(*Instant Pop. Loud.*)

(*The lights come up on the home.*)

(LINDA *enters from the kitchen, holding a mug of coffee and
a biscuit and hugging her radio. She puts the radio on its
table and slumps into the settee. There's a despair in her but
she gives nothing away.*)

PERSEPHONE (*off in kitchen*): Turn it down a bit—it's making
my head ache!

(LINDA *doesn't move.*)

Linda! . . . *Linda!*

(LINDA *moves on hand to turn the volume right up.*

PERSEPHONE *rushes on, carrying tray with cutlery and cruets,
and turns the radio off.*)

For goodness sake, you'll wake the street!

(LINDA *does not react.* PERSEPHONE *shuts door.*)

Is that all you want to eat?

(*No reply.*)

Off your food?

(*No reply.* PERSEPHONE *sighs and carries the tray to centre
table and lays a place for* RILEY.)

Well, I've still got your father to feed when he comes in.

78

It's like running a canteen in here.

(*No reply.*)

(PERSEPHONE *sighs.*)

Aren't you going to say *anything*?

LINDA: About what?

PERSEPHONE: I'm still your mother. You come in at eleven
o'clock as if you'd been out for a packet of cigarettes and
I thought you were half-way to Scotland.

LINDA: I just changed my mind, that's all.

PERSEPHONE: Did you? Why?

LINDA: Didn't fancy him.

PERSEPHONE: Well, don't tell me you did it for my sake because
I shan't thank you.

LINDA: I'm not that daft.

PERSEPHONE: You just went off him, did you?

LINDA: Yeh.

PERSEPHONE: Half-way to Scotland.

LINDA: Yes!

PERSEPHONE: You don't have to be like that. Even if you did
have a row with your boyfriend. (*Pause.*) All right then—
I'm the waitress. (*She goes over to the window.*) He'll get
wet. . . .

(*Pause.*)

I did talk to him. Before he left.

LINDA: Before he left——

PERSEPHONE: I did try. I'll have another talk with him.

LINDA: Don't bother. I don't care.

PERSEPHONE: Listen, I'm sorry it wasn't any good.

LINDA: What wasn't?

PERSEPHONE: I did hope it wouldn't be like the others.

(LINDA *is silent.*)

All right. Have it your own way.

(*She crosses to table and starts to fill the cruet from a salt
canister.* LINDA *breaks a little but not yet in her voice which
is still bitten-off.*)

LINDA: I just don't want to bore you. Turned out he was
already married. Dead simple.

PERSEPHONE: Did he tell you that?

LINDA: No, the police told me. I told you it was boring.

PERSEPHONE: The police? What happened?

LINDA: We hit a van on the motor-bike. Oh, nothing much. I didn't even fall off, but there was a couple of coppers handy, so— (*Pause, looking straight ahead.*) I thought he was giving the police a false name because he called himself something else. But he wasn't. He gave *me* that. You don't go to prison for giving people false names, only policemen, so he did it the right way round, he's no fool, is he? Yes he is, though. He asked one of the coppers on the quiet to keep me out of it because he was married, and one of them told me. Nice policeman he was. Brown eyes. I could go for him. Then I came back home.
(*Pause.*)

PERSEPHONE: Was the van driver hurt?

LINDA: There wasn't one. It was parked.
(PERSEPHONE *picks up the salt canister and goes out.* LINDA *does not move.* PERSEPHONE *returns, somewhat uncomfortable, shuts door.*)

PERSEPHONE: How—how far did you let him go?

LINDA (*after considering the question with some contempt*): Northampton. Where the hell has *he* got to?

PERSEPHONE: Pubs are over. He'll be in in a minute if I know him. Will you try not to——

LINDA: Don't worry . . . I couldn't help blowing off at him this morning. I mean, I was *right*—but——

PERSEPHONE: It's all right.

LINDA: Poor old fool. I mean, he's so bleeding ridiculous, with his suitcase and everything. It's not my fault if he has to hang around some pub like a schoolboy afraid to come home with a bad report——
(*But* PERSEPHONE *has noticed that:*)

PERSEPHONE: Oh, look what you've done!

LINDA: Listen——

PERSEPHONE: You've dropped half your supper on the carpet.

LINDA: Never mind that—
(PERSEPHONE *is already on her knees.*)
Let it be, will you——

PERSEPHONE: I can't leave it there——
LINDA (*more strained*): Look, just leave it——
PERSEPHONE: You'll tread it into the carpet.
LINDA: Mum, for God's sake will you——
PERSEPHONE: It won't take minute, move over——
  (LINDA *cracks, jumps up, throws mug on the floor.*)
LINDA (*shouting, crying*): *For Christ's sake will you please stop
  picking up my bloody crumbs!* (*And stands weeping silently.*)
  (PERSEPHONE *gets up and stands contrite.*)
  It wasn't like the others, you know, not a bit like. You
  know how old he was? Thirty. (*A great age.*) God he was
  lovely. I would have gone with him, I would really. . . .
  (*In the silence the sound of the front door.*)
PERSEPHONE: It's him. He shouldn't stay out so late.
LINDA: All those times. All that talking and loving—I thought
  I *knew* him—I thought I knew everything about him. (*She
  looks up.*) I didn't even know his name.
  (RILEY *is in the doorway.*)
RILEY: Hello, Lindy. (*Surprised and pleased.*)
LINDA: Hello.
RILEY: Oh, I am glad you're here.
PERSEPHONE: Hello, dear—just wondering where you'd got to.
  (*To* LINDA.) Bring Dad's supper in, and don't forget the
  potatoes, they're in the saucepan.
  (LINDA *goes out quickly.*)
  It's all ready for you. You must be hungry.
  (RILEY *has prepared an opening and decides to give it a try
  though he is no longer happy about it; for he has been
  expected.*)
RILEY: There was a postponement. Quite unexpected.
PERSEPHONE: Well, don't worry about that, dear.
RILEY: He had to go off. A business trip. My partner, that is.
PERSEPHONE: Well, that was bad luck.
RILEY: Yes.
  (PERSEPHONE *is not quite her normal matter-of-fact self; a
  little thrown.*)
PERSEPHONE: Well . . . put your slippers on and get comfy.
  Where are they now? Oh—

(*They're in his case.*)

I'll get them. Let's have your coat, that's right.

(PERSEPHONE *takes his coat and hat into hall and returns with case. She opens it. Takes out slippers, takes them to him.*)

Linda will have your supper in in a minute. Do you think you ought to wash your hands?

RILEY: They're not dirty.

(*He stands up and looks down on the table at the place laid for him.*)

Didn't you think I'd gone?

PERSEPHONE: Where would you go, George? Where could you go?

RILEY: Anywhere. Away. Didn't you believe any of it?

PERSEPHONE: Well——

RILEY: Because it was all true. And yet you didn't believe——

PERSEPHONE: Well, you're here now, aren't you?

RILEY: Yes, but— How did you know?

PERSEPHONE: I didn't . . . think about it.

RILEY: What I mean is . . . you laid a place for me . . . on the table. . . . (*Up.*) How did you *know*?

PERSEPHONE: Well, I know you, George. I've had time.

RILEY: Yes. . . . Yes. You've had a long time. But it *was* true.

PERSEPHONE: I'm sorry it went wrong.

RILEY: The idea was wrong.

PERSEPHONE: What idea?

RILEY: My idea. I told you.

PERSEPHONE: Did you? Which one?

RILEY: It wasn't very good.

PERSEPHONE: No, I want to know.

RILEY: It was the envelope—you remember.

PERSEPHONE: Yes—you could use it twice.

RILEY: If you had gum on both sides of the flap you could turn it inside out, you see.

PERSEPHONE: I remember.

(*Pause.*)

But wouldn't it be all torn after the first time?

(*He regards her silently.*)

RILEY: Do—do you think there was something wrong with all of them?— Something I always missed?

PERSEPHONE: Yes—yes, it's possible, isn't it? (*Pause.*) Well, I'll just take your case up for you. (*Calls.*) Linda. . . .

LINDA (*off*): All right.

(PERSEPHONE *leaves through hall.* LINDA *enters from kitchen with* RILEY'*s supper on a plate and a pot of tea. She puts them down in front of* RILEY.)

RILEY: How was Scotland?

LINDA: Bonny. How's business?

RILEY: Not too bad. Changed your mind?

LINDA: Yes.

RILEY: Well, there's lots of time. (*Pause.*) I shouldn't have gone off like that.

LINDA: Well, you're back now. Did you go to the pictures?

RILEY: No. . . . I sat in the bus station for a while. And the park. . . . It's very nice in the park. I haven't been there for a long time. Quite pretty, all the children, trees, in the middle of all the houses. . . . Have you? It's very nice. (*Pause.*) I was thinking . . . sitting there . . . in the park. . . . I mean I was thinking I wouldn't mind a change, I'm not that old . . . I was thinking perhaps I'd go down to the Labour Exchange and see . . . see what the situation is. . . . There's no harm in sounding them out.

(*The sound of rain outside is heard.*)

Might have to wait until the right thing comes along.

(*Thunder.*)

(RILEY *raises his head when he hears the thunder but goes on talking. The watering system begins to drip slowly on to the plants. They do not notice it at first.*)

But there's no harm in it, no reason why I . . . They give you a small allowance while you're waiting, while you're waiting. Assistance.

(*Louder thunder.*)

I thought I'd just walk down tomorrow and see what the situation is.

(*The noise of the dripping water increases.* LINDA *notices,*

83

*walks up to the pipes and looks at them blankly.* RILEY
*stands up, grins tiredly.*)

Oh that. . . . I'd forgotten . . . (*He speaks more strongly,
with intense pleasure.*) I'd *forgotten*!

LINDA (*levelly*): My God, it works——

RILEY (*almost jubilant, going to pipes and bathing his hands in the
water*): Well of course it works! Lindy! Indoor rain!

LINDA (*sadly dry*): Dad——

RILEY: Ah, Lindy . . .!

LINDA: Dad, is there any way of turning it off?

RILEY: What do you mean?

LINDA: I mean if it rains all night. . . .
(*Water is already spilling on the floor.*)

RILEY (*sadly*): Yes . . . yes, I see.

LINDA: I mean, if it *starts* raining when we're all asleep, and it
rains all night. . . .
(LINDA *goes off to kitchen.*)

RILEY (*alone*): Yes . . . the flaw in the ointment . . . as they say.
(*He sits down again.*) Yes. . . .
(*He tails off as* LINDA *returns with buckets and saucepans
which she distributes.* RILEY *pauses as she gets on with it.*)
Well, what I was saying was—there must be a demand for
a man of my experience. I could do . . . Oh, I could do . . .
(LINDA *has finished. She stands.*)
The trouble is, I think I was *meant* to be an inventor.
(*Pause. To* LINDA.) I'll go round tomorrow and inquire.

LINDA: Well . . . well, see how you feel.

RILEY: This little boat isn't the whole . . .
(*Pause.* LINDA *moves, quietly takes some coins out of her
purse.*)

LINDA: Got any money left. . . . (*Pause.*) I can let you have a bit
extra this week if you like. There was some overtime.

RILEY: Are you sure you'll manage?

LINDA: Yes, I'll be all right.

RILEY: Well, if you're sure. Just to tide me over. (*Takes out his
notebook and prepares to write.*) Sunday, July the sixth . . .
five shillings.
(LINDA *looks at him, hesitantly, almost shyly, grins at him.*)

*(The noise of the drips increases.)*
*(The lights fade out.)*

**CURTAIN**